# Chillir
# True Tales
# of
# Old London

## Keith Johnson

2nd Edition © Keith Johnson, 2012
First edition printed 1996

All Rights Reserved. No part of this publication may be reproduced, stored in a retrieval system, or transmitted in any form or by any means – electronic, mechanical, photocopying, recording, or otherwise – without prior written permission from the publisher.

Published by Sigma Leisure – an imprint of
Sigma Press, Stobart House, Pontyclerc, Penybanc Road
Ammanford, Carmarthenshire SA18 3HP

British Library Cataloguing in Publication Data

A CIP record for this book is available from the British Library

ISBN: 978-1-85058-891-7

Typesetting and Design by: Sigma Press, Ammanford, Carms

Printed by: Berforts Group Ltd

Every effort has been made to fulfil requirements with regard to reproducing copyright material. The author and publisher will be glad to rectify any ommissions at the earliest opportunity.

Disclaimer: The information in this book is given in good faith and is believed to be correct at the time of publication.

# Contents

# Introduction

Turn the pages of this book and embark on a journey into nineteenth century England. A century dominated by the reign of Queen Victoria which, like that of George III who occupied the throne until 1820, was to last for more than sixty years.

In all, our changing nation had four ruling monarchs during this hundred year span, with George IV holding the tenure for a decade and William IV spending seven years in the exalted position. Under their care the country was to become the manufacturing capital of the world.

Raw materials were shipped to a Britain which alone possessed the machines and human-skill to turn them into goods which the world desired. Increased trade led to the necessary improvements in transportation, and canals, roads and railway tracks all developed with unbridled haste. The cotton trade, coal and iron manufacture accounted for a huge portion of the nations work force. The attraction of the mills and mines was money, and those hardy enough endured long hours for low pay in the 'workshop of the world'.

The British excelled in business, with money to invest at home and abroad. They had the added confidence of the best developed banking system and the world's most stable government.

The Census taken in 1851 revealed that half the population of 21 million had taken up residence in the towns and cities. Although agriculture was, at the time, still Britain's greatest industry, the people were flocking into the textile and heavy industrial areas.

From the beginning of the century the population of Great Britain had almost doubled and the greatest density of population was in the eastern part of London, a capital city with close to 2 million residents. In the most populated area almost two hundred thousand people lived in a square mile.

It is not surprising, therefore, that in 1853 an article appeared in the press that shocked the nation. Under the heading 'The Health of London', it was revealed that upwards of a thousand deaths were recorded in the metropolis weekly. The common saying was that 'the large towns were the graves of the people' and the high rate of mortality prevalent amongst large assemblages of human beings was regarded as a regrettable, but unavoidable, product of city life. It was felt that the mortality rate was at least double what it should have been had a satisfactory sanitary system been in place.

Five hundred people a week, many young and innocent, were consigned prematurely to the reeking grave and the over full pest house. The deaths were not the work of some midnight assassin, but carried out in broad daylight in every narrow court and alleyway, in the vicinity of every open ditch and obstructed sewer. Within a stone's throw of the stateliest habitations, where the killer seldom attacked, the undertaker was huddling up the work to make room for more slaughter.

The gully-hole, which inadequately attempted to convey the filth away from the humble houses, was the den of a whole troop of assassins. The foul agents issuing forth entered the dwellings and blasted the health and the hopes of whole families at once, for if the head of the family was the victim, what but pauperism, or beggary, or worse was left for the survivors? Once stricken by the fever, the victim, if he survived the attack, carried the results with him to the grave, in the shape of a debilitated constitution or a depressed physical and moral energy.

Further sources of reeking pestilence were the pools of filthy water, heaps of rotting vegetables, dead dogs and cats and every imaginable variety of domestic refuse, enthroned on muck heaps. Instead of the cellars draining into the streets, the streets drained into the cellars and not even an apology for a sewer existed.

The same description applied to thousands of places within a few yards of every public thoroughfare in the metropolis. As a consequence, out of the whole population of London rather more than forty out of every thousand died annually. The victims perished due to neglect and indifference, as if they had been abandoned to the tender mercies of the assassin or the thug. The task was to rid the land of the army of devastators, whose chief was typhus and whose ally was cholera. The plea was for the mass of the people to have access to the good sanitary conditions enjoyed by those more fortunate and favoured.

Crime, like the poor, is always with us, and although less prevalent than a century before, the fear of violence and plunder was always in the mind. The 'evil-disposed' person still infested the private lanes and passages, the public streets and places of usual concourse.

In the eighteenth century a foul host of rogues and blackguards had preyed upon the denizens of the country. Among them were the highwaymen, who were often portrayed as the aristocrats of their profession. Pocket-picking was reduced to a fine art and the light-fingered gentry plied their trade dextrously in every busy street. The footpad lurked in every side street and alley, ready to enforce his demands with brutal violence.

When the nineteenth century unfolded, the situation in London, and other densely populated regions, was that villainy and every variety of vice was prevalent. In the capital city there were over five thousand public houses and beer shops, many of which were the meeting places of highwaymen, housebreakers, cardsharps and counterfeit coiners.

London alone was the base for fifty or more mints engaged in counterfeit coining, one of which produced some £200,000 worth of bad half-crowns in seven years. Burglary and housebreaking were daily occurrences and the citizen's only defence was a stout cudgel or a brace of pistols.

There was no police force, or at least none of any consequence. What law enforcement there was acted both inefficiently and corruptly. The Watch, which nightly patrolled the streets with their staves and lanterns, was for the most part composed of aged, decrepit, infirm dodderers who seemed to keep well out of the way when villainy was being performed

The authorities often had to rely on the informer to prosecute the ends of justice, and after pointing the finger, the informer was given a monetary reward. Such was the English Law the nineteenth century inherited, that over two hundred offences were punishable by death.

The Law in its severity, in fact, terrified those who administered it as much as those who fell foul of it. Judges pounced on every technical irregularity as an excuse for acquittal and juries were ever conscious of the fate awaiting those they found guilty. As a result, the condemned often had the Royal power of Clemency exercised in their favour, and male convicts were pardoned in large numbers whenever England was at war.

Eventually, between 1825 and 1829, Sir Robert Peel drastically reformed the criminal code and brought about a system of certain, rather than savage, punishment. The emergence of the new forces of law and order, initially in the metropolis, led to a feeling of increased security for those who resided in its boundaries. The top hatted law enforcers, inevitably nicknamed the 'Peelers', gave the people a greater feeling of security in a volatile world.

By the middle of the century there were, nation-wide, over two hundred and fifty prisons and these housed in the region of thirty thousand people of all descriptions. The prison cells were occupied by many, who a decade or two before, would have suffered death for their crimes. Many others, though, had been transported as felons, to distant colonies, a practice begun in the reign of Elizabeth, and set to continue until the sixtieth year of the century.

Perhaps a greater reflection on society in the middle of the century was the fact that over four times the prison population were housed in the nations 748 workhouses. It was only in 1833 that the first national grant for education was made, that consisting of the lavish sum of £20,000. Hitherto, what crumbs of learning the poor had managed to pick up were the gifts of self sacrificing individuals with an urge for social reform. In a time of poverty and degradation, it was deemed more useful for a scantily clad child to toil in a coal mine, working in an atmosphere often less wholesome than a sewer. The ends to which the poor were reduced for sake of food almost exceeded belief.

This was the stage on which the criminals acted out their crimes, and it is against their background that judgement should be made in these more enlightened times.

The Church and the Chapel, the reformer and the temperate, all gave hope to those who toiled daily against adversity. Much kindness flowed from within those human hearts, and passionate belief unlocked the shackles of mediocrity.

From misery the kindly souls made happiness, yet dwelling amongst them were the desperate, the determined and the devious, all acting out their roles.

Whether they be pilferers, poisoners or pretenders, or, in fact rogues, rioters or ruffians, they all in their time were destined for the limelight.

The dramas they enacted often had a violent or traumatic end, and on many occasions the all too eager executioner was ready to bring down the curtain on another tragic tale. They were crowded years, and the tales contained in the following chapters recall some of the events that shocked and saddened the inhabitants of our streets, more than a century ago.

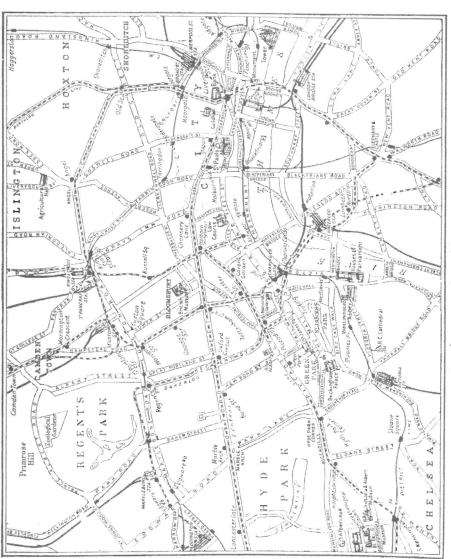

*London: a city shaped by its past*

# Acknowledgements

I am indebted to the journalists of a bygone era who described the events that took place in great detail. The reporters of the national, regional and London newspapers deserve praise for their accounts of the past that helped to make this book possible. I am also indebted to the following publications for the manner in which they chronicled events of the past: *The Illustrated London News; The Strand Magazine; Leisure Hour Magazine; Newgate Calendar.* I further acknowledge the assistance given me by the staff of the Harris Reference Library in Preston and other libraries throughout the country – they are quite wonderful.

My thanks go to Patricia Crook who put her literary skills, time and cheerful encouragement at my disposal. I will remain forever grateful.

My thanks are extended to Glen Crook for his enthusiastic commitment to the book's photographic requirements and to J.C. Fielding for providing the line drawings and sketches that accompany the varies chapters.

# Attempt to Assassinate The Queen

In 1837, King William IV died and was succeeded by his niece, Victoria, who was, at the time, eighteen years old. The country had been ruled by a succession of ageing kings, and the reign of Victoria was greeted with much enthusiasm. The slight, fair-haired, blue-eyed young lady with a pretty complexion was cheered everywhere she went by appreciative crowds. She radiated happiness and seemed delighted that she had found herself the greatest and most important sovereign in the world.

Victoria was full of pride in her country. She began her reign while a Tsar ruled Russia, an Emperor controlled Austria and Kings and Princes held power in Italy and Germany. The nation was anxious for her to stay on the throne, the next heir being her uncle, the Duke of Cumberland, a most unpopular son of George III. For fear that she may die without children, great activity took place to arrange her future marriage partner. As a result, in the autumn of 1839, Prince Albert of Saxe-Coburg-Gotha visited England.

Fortunately, Victoria became fond of the Prince and in February, 1840 they were married. The wedding was a great relief to those in high circles, and the serious-minded and clever Prince Albert soon became a good companion to her.

*The young Victoria and Prince Albert*

The Queen freely appeared in public, confident of her security amongst the affectionate and loyal people, despite the fact that reigning monarchs down the years had been the victims of various outrages. In 1786, a mad woman, Margaret Nicholson, had tried to stab George II at the gates of St James's Palace and, in 1800, a discharged soldier fired a pistol at him from the pit of Drury Lane Theatre. Queen Victoria's immediate predecessor, William IV, was the victim of a murderous outrage on Ascot race-course in 1832, when Dennis Collins, dressed in the garb of a sailor, threw a stone at the King which hit him on the forehead.

Sadly, Her Majesty's trust in her subjects was to be dealt a severe blow in June 1840. On the tenth day of the month, at about quarter past six o'clock, Her Majesty and Prince Albert left Buckingham Palace for an evening drive in Hyde Park prior to dinner. The carriage, a low open vehicle drawn by four horses ridden by postilions, passed the crowds gathered at the gates and made its way up Constitution Hill.

Before the royal couple had travelled very far, a man appeared at the side of their carriage and, putting his hand upon his breast, produced a pistol from beneath his lapel. In the next instant he aimed it at the Queen and discharged it in her direction. Aware of the danger, Prince Albert pulled Her Majesty down in the carriage and, as he did so, the assailant produced a second pistol and once more took aim and fired. The discharged pistol ball whistled over the heads of the crouching couple with the Prince shielding the Queen with his body. The carriage at once began to gather speed and Victoria and Albert were soon out of range of their would-be assassin.

The discharge of the pistols had been very loud, and several people at once rushed towards the perpetrator of the gross outrage and he was immediately

*Pistol wielding Edward Oxford confronted the royal couple*

seized. The royal couple appeared unruffled by their traumatic experience and continued with their evening drive, calling at the Duchess of Kent's home in Belgrave Square. They returned to Buckingham Palace within the hour, showing no apparent alarm over the deadly attack from which they had providentially escaped.

The man detained for the crime was nineteen year old Edward Oxford who had lodgings in West Street, West Square. His lodgings, which constituted of only a bedroom, were minutely searched by the police, but nothing was found except a copy of rules and regulations of some supposed secret society and a sword. The pistols were described as small, of Birmingham manufacture and rather well finished. One of the discharged balls was said to have struck the wall opposite, and the other was believed to have lodged in a tree.

Edward Oxford was said to be naturally of a sullen, perverse and turbulent disposition, a person quite unable to repress the violence of his passions. He had been born in Birmingham and, as a lad, had travelled to London. Most of his working life had been as a bar man in local public houses including the 'Kings Head Inn' at Hounslow, which his aunt had kept. About two years previously he had appeared before the Magistrates at Brentford, where he had been fined for his part in a brawl during which, with the use of a clasp knife, he had inflicted a severe wound on one youth.

While in custody young Oxford expressed little anxiety or concern and he seemed to have a craze for notoriety. After his arrest he thought only of the excitement his assassination attempt had raised, and not of the fatal consequences that may have ensued.

In the first week of July 1840, he appeared at the Central Criminal Court charged with High Treason. As he entered the crowded court room he gazed with complacency at the large gathering. Having made a survey of the assembly, he leaned upon the front of the dock, resting on his elbows. When the indictment was read he replied in a firm tone, 'Not Guilty', and dismissed the charge with loud and discordant fits of laughter.

As the proceedings progressed, it was revealed that Oxford had purchased the pistols for £2 from premises in Blackfriars Road and that during the weeks prior to the outrage, he had been practising his shooting at various shooting galleries in the city, including those at Leicester Square and in the Strand.

Despite previous reports to the contrary, it was stated that the balls from the pistols had not been found and the defence laboured on this point, suggesting that the pistols may not have been loaded. Oxford's rather unusual behaviour, in the court and following his arrest, was felt, by the defence, to bear out a plea of insanity. Consequently they dwelt on the possibility of hereditary insanity, claiming that his grandfather had been detained for a number of years in the mental wards of Greenwich Hospital, and that his father had been at times quite mad and a man of violent passions.

Reference was made to the papers found in his lodgings which related to a secret society. They were the rules of an association called 'Young England'. This was said not to exist, being only a fictitious organisation dreamed up by the young offender. Sworn members, according to the regulations, were honour bound to provide themselves with sword, rifle, dagger and a pair of pistols and, if required, to go into the country on the business of the association. In all, they were said to be the manifest inventions of a disordered intellect.

The proceedings had begun at nine o'clock in the morning and the jury retired at a quarter past five o'clock, with his Lordship asking them to seek a verdict that would give satisfaction to their own minds, and an example to future jurors. Within the hour the jury had returned. When they delivered their verdict it caused a good deal of surprise in the court, the foreman stating – "We find the prisoner guilty of discharging two pistols at Her Majesty, but whether they were loaded with ball or not is not satisfactorily or sufficiently proved, he being at the time in an unsound state of mind".

The announcement left the Defence Counsel seeking acquittal and, after lengthy discussions, the jury were ordered to once again retire and reconsider their verdict. This they did and, in about another hour, returned to state that Edward Oxford was 'Guilty', being at the time insane.

The Attorney General asked the court to order that the prisoner be put in some place of safe custody until Her Majesty's pleasure be known respecting him. His Lordship then stated that the Order would be made in due course. Edward Oxford was subsequently removed from the dock having shown no emotion on hearing the verdict.

Initially he was detained in Newgate Gaol and then, on a warrant from the Secretary of State, admitted to Bethlem Hospital. When the great criminal lunatic asylum was opened at Broadmoor, he was transferred there. In 1878 he was released from that institution and he immediately went to live abroad.

**Postscript**
In the years that followed other murderous attempts were made on the life of Queen Victoria, but she was unbowed by them and became one of history's great survivors. She lived until January 1901, to end the longest and, in some ways, the greatest reign that this country has ever known.

Sadly the life of Prince Albert was much shorter. He died at Windsor in 1861 and the Queen, who was devoted to him, was heartbroken.

# 'Young England'

## Rules and Regulations

1. That every member shall be provided with a brace of pistols, a sword, a rifle, and a dagger. The two latter to be kept at the committee-room.

2. That every member must, on entering, take the oath of allegiance to be true to the cause he has joined.

3. That every member must, on entering the house, give a signal to the sentry.

4. That every officer shall have a fictitious name. His right name and address to be kept with the secretary.

5. That every member shall, when he is ordered to meet, be armed with a brace of pistols (loaded) and a sword to repel any attack; and also be provided with a black crape cap, to cover his face with – his marks of distinction outside.

6. That whenever any member wishes to introduce any new member, he must give satisfactory accounts of him to their superiors, and from thence to the council.

7. Any member who can procure a hundred men shall be promoted to the rank of captain.

8. Any member holding communications with any country agents must instantly forward the intelligence to the secretary.

9. That whenever any member is ordered down the country or abroad, he must take various disguises with him (as the labourer, the mechanic, and the gentleman), all of which he can obtain at the committee-room.

10. That any member wishing to absent himself for more than one month must obtain leave from the commander-in-chief.

11. That no member will be allowed to speak during any debate, nor allowed to ask more than two questions.

All the printed rules to be kept at the Committee-room.

*Rules of Edward Oxford's secret society 'Young England'*

# Captain Montgomery's Acid Alternative

In the early part of the nineteenth century, the crime of uttering forged bank notes was often punished by execution, although in many cases the convicts were spared from the gallows, and given instead lengthy terms of imprisonment or transported for life.

There was, therefore, great interest in the proceedings at the Old Bailey at the end of June, 1828 when four men, James Anderson, George Morris, William Rice and Captain John Montgomery, stood accused of that crime. All four were found guilty and sentenced to execution on Friday, July 4th of that year.

The verdicts and sentences led to a great deal of activity and pleas for Royal clemency. Within hours, Anderson and Morris heard that their executions had been respited. For Rice and Montgomery the news was less favourable, and they both faced the forfeiture of their life for their forgery activities.

Captain Montgomery, who was in his late thirties, had been a familiar character on the London scene, mixing in good society. Born in the County of Kildare, some fifteen miles from Dublin, he was the son of a corn and flour merchant who was a landowner of some distinction. His father, who was an influential man in Dublin, obtained a Commission for him in a foot regiment. It was hoped that life in the army would help the reckless youth to settle down, but he soon quitted his position. On resigning, however, he took care to retain his nominal rank as Captain, a title by which he was ever after known.

It was claimed that, in Dublin, he became adept at forgery and counterfeited the signature of a leading citizen. The man had written in an extremely cramped and illegible hand, and the imitation was so perfect that the forged signatures could not be told from the legal ones. In the end, the matter was overlooked, thanks in no small way to Captain Montgomery's father who wished his family to retain their respectability.

After his arrival in London, cheating and swindling became a daily occurrence for him. On one occasion, after forging documents to a banking house, he was pursued by the officials, and only by delivering up the fruits of his villainy, plus watches and trinkets, did he avoid prosecution. Eventually, however, he ended up in the debtor's side of Newgate Prison and after frequent visits there, he spent three years in the criminal prison as his forgery came to light.

After his liberation he resolved to mend his ways, moving into the country and elevating his status from Captain to Colonel, a rank held by one of his two brothers. His deceitful ways almost paid off, as he planned marriage to the daughter of a respectable gentleman. Unfortunately for him, the marriage did not take place when his true identity was discovered.

Upon his return to London, he received an unfriendly welcome from tradesmen who were somewhat reluctant to give him credit. In consequence, and as a last resort, he took to the circulation of forged bank notes. His transactions became so numerous and frequent that the tradesmen could only wonder at his extraordinary nerve in continuing his reckless action. His apprehension was inevitable and his sentence the expected one.

Before he retired on his last night, he wrote two letters. One letter was to a friend whom he told of his readiness to exchange to another world, and the other letter was to the prison surgeon, Mr. Box. In that letter he bequeathed his body to the surgeon for dissection in the hope that the profession would benefit from it, and he begged that Mr. Box would have the goodness to preserve his heart in spirits and give it to a young female to whom he was fondly attached.

When he had finished the letters he was locked up by the turnkeys in the usual manner, and when they bade him goodnight he appeared very composed.

*In the summer of 1828, Captain Montgomery was tried at London's Old Bailey*

At six o'clock the following morning the turnkeys returned to the cell and, when they unlocked it, found him stretched on his back on the bed. He lay completely naked with his eyes and mouth open. It was soon apparent that the cold body was deprived of life. A small bottle containing a few drops of prussic acid was discovered near the body.

Further investigation ascertained that he had taken as much as would kill a horse in a few minutes and the composure of his features suggested that he had not suffered much pain.

Despite the discovery the prison governor still had the matter of William Rice's execution to deal with. At a few minutes before eight o'clock, that unfortunate youth was led from his cell into the press room. The awful procession then moved slowly on to the gallows, the steps of which he ascended with great fortitude.

After a few minutes engaged in prayer, the drop fell, and Rice was launched into eternity, appearing to die without a struggle. News of the death of Montgomery had not reached the immense crowd gathered outside and they attributed his absence to a respite of sentence.

The next day an inquest was held in the upper press room of Newgate Gaol into the death of Captain Montgomery. The hearing was told that the body had been opened. The stomach was found to be in a highly inflamed state and that the vessels about the head and neck were gorged with blood. From the stomach, a quantity of prussic acid was extracted, this being of sufficient quantity to cause death in a few minutes.

Read out at the inquest were the contents of a couple of the letters he had written on the day before his death. One was to a female to whom he was evidently warmly attached and included the following extract:

"One more last farewell, one more last adieu, to a being so much attached to the unhappy Montgomery. Oh, my dearest girl. If it had been in the power of anyone to avert my dreadful doom, your kind exertions would have been attended with success.

Oh, God! So poor Montgomery is to die upon the scaffold. How dreadful have been my hours of reflection, whilst in this dreary cell. The bitterness of my reflection is bitter in the extreme. How I wished to have disappointed the horrid multitude who will be assembled to witness my ignominious exit.

Farewell for ever.

J.B. Montgomery "

At the end of the proceedings the jury returned a verdict that the deceased had poisoned himself by taking a quantity of prussic acid when in a state of sanity. To which the coroner replied that it was, therefore, a case of *felo de se.*

Montgomery's remains were interred at ten o'clock on the Saturday night in the churchyard adjoining St. Sepulchre's Church. The law specifying that in all cases of *felo de se* the deceased must be interred between the hours of nine and twelve at night. There were, of course, no religious observations or prayers for the deceased.

# A Doomed Conspiracy Hatched in Cato Street

During the final days of February, 1820, as the nation was coming to terms with the death of King George III, the country was informed of a horrible conspiracy to assassinate His Majesty's ministers. The plot, with its unmitigated wickedness of design, has no parallel in the annals of our history since the Gun Powder Treason, in the reign of King James I.

A diabolical conspiracy had been going on for some time, and the man behind it was the notorious Arthur Thistlewood. During his life he had been in considerable trouble with the authorities for his mischievous pursuits.

On one occasion he had stood trial on a charge of high treason and been acquitted. On another he was imprisoned for his violent conduct towards Lord Sidmouth. The noble Lord had suffered repeated insults and been challenged to a duel by Thistlewood. For his outrageous actions he was tried, found guilty and sentenced to a long term of imprisonment in Horsham gaol. From this situation he obtained an early release, thanks to the humane intervention of Lord Sidmouth.

No sooner did Thistlewood breath the air of liberty than he joined his former companions, whose spirit seemed to revive at the presence of their leader. A deluded man, he still entertained a hope that there were those, like himself, who, driven from society by their crimes, were capable of undertaking any enterprise, however diabolical. Houses were opened in various parts of London at which the 'radical fraternity', as they were called, held their nightly orgies. On these occasions the most dreadful vengeance was denounced against particular individuals, and a period anticipated when these threats should be realised with a fatal certainty.

As things transpired, every step taken by the conspirators was known to the ministry. Agents were employed to watch the progress of these alarming individuals. Many, after being persuaded to join the society, and on discovering the horrible deeds contemplated, were the first to give information that might lead to their frustration.

Consequently the ministers learnt, a few days prior to its enactment, of a plot to assassinate them. A public dinner was planned by Lord Harrowby at his Grosvenor Square home. The cabinet were to attend, and this was seen by Thistlewood as the ideal opportunity to carry into execution his diabolical design.

In preparation, the plotters took over premises in the west end of town, in Cato Street, Edgware Road. The premises, in a dilapidated state, consisted of a stable with stalls for three horses with a loft above which was only accessible by a ladder. On Wednesday, 23rd February, the day publicly announced for the dinner, the conspirators were actively engaged in collecting arms and ammunition necessary for their infernal enterprise.

The first precautionary step taken was to transfer the proposed cabinet gathering to the Earl of Liverpool's home. The servants of Lord Harrowby were instructed to keep up the semblance of preparation. It was next resolved to arrest the criminals, and the Magistrate of Bow Street was enlisted to supervise the hazardous undertaking. Fifteen police officers and a company of the Coldstream Guards were under his instructions. Soon after the close of day, the Magistrate, armed with a warrant for the arrest of Arthur Thistlewood and twelve others upon a charge of felony, set off on his expedition. Some of the men carried pistols and cutlasses, but others were only provided with their staves of office.

Arriving at the scene, the Magistrate posted most of his men in the 'Horse and Groom' public house and, concealing himself, kept an eye on the conspirators' den. He observed several persons passing backwards and forwards to the premises and, becoming apprehensive that the postponement or removal of the dinner had been discovered, he therefore resolved to commence his operations.

A messenger was sent to summon the approach of the Guards and, after allowing what he thought sufficient time to ensure their support, he advanced with his little band, which included several elderly men.

On arriving at the stable door, they found it locked and had to use force to open it. A sentinel stood at the foot of the ladder leading to the loft and they secured him, but not before he had passed the word of 'an enemy' to his associates above. At once the gallant officers mounted the ladder and, on reaching the loft, they saw a body of some thirty men, all busily employed in loading fire-arms, filling hand grenades and generally preparing for combat.

The cry, "We are peace-officers, lay down your arms," greeted the conspirators, and in a moment all was confusion. Thistlewood responded by advancing with a long cut and thrust sword and seemed determined to resist the pistol wielding intruders. Ordered to drop his sword or be fired upon, he lunged forward and in an instant had slain one of the officers, Richard Smithers. As the man lay dying a pistol was fired at Thistlewood, and the leader of the conspirators responded by ordering his men to extinguish the lights. The scene then became utterly appalling with the plotters firing at the officers and out of the windows into the street. Intent on making good his escape, Thistlewood forced his way down the ladder and, despite receiving a pistol wound in his left hand, made a hasty exit into the street.

Many of the officers were wounded as an incessant fire was reigned upon them and it became apparent that several of the would be assassins were escaping through a back route. Much later than anticipated, the Guards arrived, and immediately the Magistrate ordered them to surround the building. A desperate conflict followed, but darkness had favoured the escape of many of the wretches and, at its conclusion, only nine of them were captured.

They were instantly handcuffed together, placed in hackney coaches and taken to the police offices in Bow Street, under a strong military escort. On arrival the Magistrate took his seat upon The Bench and prepared to examine the prisoners.

*The conspirators were confronted by the officers of the law*

Among those at the bar was James Ings, a butcher, a short, squat man who had, next to Thistlewood, made the most desperate resistance. He exhibited a most terrific appearance – flushed and heated from the struggle, his hands, face and clothes were besmeared with blood, and his small, fiery eyes glared, with a satanic expression, at the spectators. The beholders turned aside with horror, a feeling which was aggravated when, asked his occupation by the Magistrate, Ings replied in a strong, harsh voice, "Me? I was bred to the butchering business".

Besides the butcher there were four shoe or boot makers, three carpenters or cabinet makers and a tailor. All were said to have been prominently active in the affray. They were, for the most part, men of short stature, mean exterior and unmarked physiognomy, the exception being the cabinet maker, William Davidson, who was described as a man of colour.

The office was crowded with soldiers and officers bringing in arms and ammunition of various kinds. There were muskets, carbines, broad-swords, pistols, blunderbusses, cartridges, gun powder and all other items that a revolutionary body would require.

Tales of heroism, bravery and daring were relayed and considerable number of officers presented evidence against the captured conspirators. The interrogation of the prisoners went on into the night, and before it broke up the Magistrate ordered an extraordinary gazette to be published, offering a thousand pounds reward for the apprehension of Thistlewood.

Within hours, private information was given that Thistlewood had retired to a house in White Street, Moorfields. A body of officers was at once despatched to apprehend him. The house was searched and the man was located in a room on the ground floor. The entrance of the officers woke him from his slumbers and, appearing somewhat dispirited, he assured them he would make no resistance.

After searching the apartment, the officers placed Thistlewood in a hackney-coach and he was conveyed to Bow Street. On his way the carriage was followed by a crowd of people who repeatedly cried out, "Hang the villain! Hang the assassin," and other exclamations of a similar nature.

The news of his arrest was heard with infinite satisfaction and persons of the highest rank were keen to learn the particulars of what had transpired. Appearing before the Magistrate, he wore an old, black coat and waistcoat, which were threadbare; a pair of corduroy breeches, very much worn; and old worsted stockings. As he sat, handcuffed, his dark eyes turned upon the spectators and his appearance was wretched to the extreme.

Thistlewood's apprehension was not the final one, others followed during the next few days. Among those taken was a man of the name Brunt, said to be second in command to Thistlewood. A vast quantity of hand grenades and other combustibles were found in his room.

On the following Sunday morning, as early as ten o'clock, all the great avenues to the west end of the town leading to Cato Street, were lined with persons of every rank and description. They pressed forward with the utmost eagerness to take a view of the stable and loft wherein the horrible plot was planned, and where the unfortunate Smithers had met with his death. The horror it had excited throughout the metropolis could not easily be described. The stable and loft was shown at so much per head, and the doors of a theatre were never more anxiously besieged for admittance than the Cato Street gangs hide-out. By four o'clock in the afternoon upwards of £50 had been taken in admission money by those who owned the stable. The 'Horse and Groom' public house, where the body of Smithers had lain, was crowded to excess until a late hour.

The trial of the conspirators took place six weeks later at the Old Bailey. Thistlewood made a long and rambling defence, the chief features of it being abuse of Lord Sidmouth, and the vilification of an informer named Edwards. Several other prisoners took the same line towards Edwards, and there seemed to be good reason for supposing that he was a greater villain than any of those arraigned.

He had been in a state of abject poverty when he first became acquainted with the conspirators, with neither a bed to lie on nor a coat upon his back. His situation changed dramatically when he took up the profitable role as Government informer and spy, and for some time he appeared to have supported both sides. In the words of Thistlewood, he was described as a "contriver, instigator and entrapper," and it was said that he incited the associates he was betraying to commit outrage.

Inevitably the trial concluded with Lord Chief Justice Abbot placing the black velvet cap on his head and proceeding to his awful duty, addressing the prisoners thus:

"You, Arthur Thistlewood, James Ings, John Thomas Brunt, William Davidson and Richard Tidd, have been severally tried and convicted of High Treason, in compassing and levying war against His Majesty.

You, James Wilson, John Harrison, Richard Bradburn, John Shaw Strange, James Gilchrist and Charles Cooper, did originally plead not guilty to the indictment; but after trial and conviction of the preceding prisoners, you desired to withdraw your pleas and plead guilty. You have cast yourselves on the mercy of your Sovereign, and if any of you have your lives spared I hope you will bear in mind that you owe it to the benignity and mercy of your Sovereign".

Continuing with his address, he reminded the convicted men of their actions. They had intended to take away the lives of fourteen of His Majesty's ministers with a crime that was a stranger to this country. He concluded by pronouncing the sentence of the law in the following manner:

"That you, and each of you, be taken from hence to the gaol from whence you came, and from thence that you be drawn upon a hurdle to a place of execution, and there be hanged by the neck until you be dead; and afterwards your heads shall be severed from your bodies and your bodies be divided into four quarters, to be disposed of as His Majesty shall think fit. And may God in his infinite goodness have mercy upon your souls".

In the days that followed, Wilson, Harrison, Bradburn, Strange, Gilchrist and Cooper were told that their sentences were respited; and all except Gilchrist informed that they were to be transported for life.

Finally, on May Day, 1820, the dreadful sentence of the law was executed upon Thistlewood, Ings, Tidd, Davidson and Brunt at the usual place of execution, in front of the Old Bailey. The scaffold was erected in front of the Debtor's door, but made of larger dimensions to admit space for the coffins of the wretched sufferers, and room for the blocks on which the heads were to be removed from the bodies after they had been suspended for half an hour.

From the early hours of the morning, the crowds flooded to the execution scene and a guinea was given, without hesitation, for any place which gave a clear view of the scaffold. Troops were stationed at each end of the Old Bailey, and also distributed in other parts of the city for the duration of the executions.

All the condemned men were said to have spent a good night and Thistlewood had slept from midnight until four in the morning. They had all been visited in the course of the previous evening by the chaplain of Newgate gaol, but all except Davidson, the man of colour, disregarded the salutary advice of the chaplain. When the chaplain returned at six o'clock in the morning, Davidson received the sacrament and implored pardon from the Almighty for his transgressions. His example was, however, rejected by the other prisoners who avowed themselves

Deists and declined the proffered assistance from any minister of religion.

Thistlewood was offered a glass of wine, which he politely declined, but took a glass of water and a biscuit; the other prisoners also partaking of some light refreshment.

Shortly before seven-thirty, the men were taken, one by one, from their respective cells into the prison yard to have their irons struck off on a block prepared for the purpose. Thistlewood was taken into the yard by three men and he looked thin and pale, being dressed in the same clothes as at the trial, with his coat buttoned close up. He seemed, however, perfectly cool and collected and, looking up to the sky, he remarked to the person next to him that it seemed a fine morning. The last man brought into the yard was Davidson reading aloud from a prayer book in his hands. After speaking to his unfortunate companions, he uttered prayers with the utmost fervency.

The prisoners were then conducted in the usual form to the scaffold, which they mounted it in the order in which they had entered the prison yard. As soon as Thistlewood ascended he bowed to the multitude with great composure and addressed a few words to them. They were, in substance, that he had endeavoured to do well for his countrymen, and hoped they would consider he had done his duty.

When Ings stepped on to the scaffold he tried to excite three cheers, but it had no effect on the immense multitude who, observing the dreadful spectacle, became silent. Ings immediately followed his attempt to cheer by singing aloud the first two lines of the popular song "Give me death or liberty".

As the pinioning stage progressed, Tidd drew the cap over his own eyes and adjusted the rope without the aid of the executioner. Brunt maintained the same composure and said he would rather die a thousand deaths than live in slavery.

The preparatory business of the executioner lasted nearly quarter of an hour. The fatal drop then fell, and the wretched sufferers were launched into eternity at five minutes past eight o'clock. The struggles of Ings and Brunt were protracted for several minutes, but the other prisoners seemed to die in almost a moment.

After the bodies had been suspended for half an hour, they were cut down and fell into the coffins prepared for them. One of the executioners then proceeded to carry into effect the next part of the dreadful sentence by cutting off the heads from the bodies. This was performed by a man dressed in sailor's clothes with his face covered by black crepe. He commenced by raising up Thistlewood's body and placing it on the block. He then severed the head from the body with anatomical adroitness, using a large knife. Holding the head up in his hand, he then proclaimed it, by name, the head of a traitor. The same dreadful ceremony was repeated with the four other heads. That part of the sentence which directed the bodies should be quartered was remitted.

The whole business of the execution occupied about three-quarters of an hour, after which time the bodies were removed into the gaol, and the immense crowd began to disperse.

*The heads of the conspirators were shown to the crowds*

## Postscript
The Government were not particularly proud of their agent, the informer Edwards, and, after the convictions had been assured, he was sent abroad. He was said to have been given an ample pension, on condition that he did not return to England.

# The Morn The Theatre Roof Fell In

On the last Thursday in February, 1828, the new Royal Brunswick Theatre in Wellclose Square, London was the scene of much activity. Approximately one hundred were busily employed in the theatre that day. Some were putting the finishing touches to the building, which had cost upwards of £20,000, while others were on the stage, preparing to be cast for roles in the opera *Guy Mannering*.

Suddenly, without warning, disaster struck. The roof of the building collapsed and with it fell the wall which fronted on to Well Street. Many bricks and timbers were flung into the street, and a passing drayman had his dray and two horses crushed beneath the falling masonry.

Within minutes the cloud of dust had settled and only three sides of the theatre's shell remained standing, beneath the mangled structure the fight for survival was underway. Many had miraculously avoided serious injury and amongst them were those intent on saving others. They emerged from their perilous predicament to relate their stories.

One such man, named Shaw, had been employed in the counting house, forty feet above the stage, when the collapse occurred. In an instant he had found himself and his wife below the stage with a large plank, across their bodies. Extricating himself from beneath the plank he carried his wife up a staircase and, having gained a window, lowered her into the street by a rope before making his own escape. Both were a little bruised but, in the circumstances, happy to be alive.

The stage manager, Mr. Farren, had been in the proprietor's box when the roof fell in. Only a beam saved him from being crushed. He remained a considerable time in the awful situation and eventually observed some movement nearby, in the heap of rubble that covered the stage. The movement was made by a young lady, fifteen years of age and, stretching out his hand, he was able to draw her into the box. Realising that they remained in peril, he summoned his resolve and led her to safety by a dangerous passage over a heap of shifting ruins.

When news of the catastrophe spread, the district Magistrates assembled and a body of labourers were enlisted from the St. Catherine Dock to clear away the immense pile of bricks and timber. From beneath the rubble could be heard the voices of unfortunate sufferers. The dock labourers were directed by Mr. Hardwick, the architect of the dock, whose endeavours to save life were unremitting. He seemed to care little for his own safety, crossing over the most dangerous places and, at one point, being struck upon the chest when a portion of the ruin gave way.

In the course of the day the labourers recovered half a dozen bodies from beneath the ruins and also rescued twice that number who had been trapped and unable to free themselves. Each one that emerged with broken limbs or more serious injuries was immediately conveyed to hospital.

Amongst those reported dead was the proprietor of the theatre, Mr. Maurice, who was not killed in the theatre but outside in the street. Rushing out of the building, he had placed himself as he thought, out of harm's way. Unfortunately, some large brickbats from the falling ruin knocked him down and he was crushed to death beneath a heap of falling masonry.

Only at a late hour did rescue work cease for the day and, at an early hour on the Friday morning, the search was restarted. It had been reported that all the musicians were buried under the rubble and that cries could be heard from the orchestra pit. Indeed, it was claimed that one musician had been heard beating a drum. This, fortunately, proved to be no more than an absurd exaggeration when rescue workers were eventually able to search that area. In fact, throughout the day only one body was discovered, that of a carpenter called William Leader who had been crushed beneath falling timber.

On the Saturday morning a list of those killed was issued. Besides the theatre proprietor, Mr. Maurice, a further eleven victims were recorded. These included three carpenters, a door keeper from the theatre, a blacksmith and a fruit salesman.

Amongst those who witnessed the tragedy was the Rev. Smith of Penzance who was one of the first people at the scene and spent the entire day tendering assistance to the sufferers. He recalled the event in the following manner:

"I called on everyone to help directly, which they did with all promptitude, and in an instant after removing a few planks we found a man partly sitting and alive. He was at once hurried to his home.

I then saw a female figure emerging from the far end of the ruins, she was filled with horror, not knowing what to do; some men ran to her and helped her over the rubble. Her hair was dishevelled, her clothes torn and her face covered with blood. She was helped to safety crying out how grateful she was to be alive. I then hastened over to the part of the theatre where a faint noise was heard and there, under the stage beams in a hole, half buried with rubbish we found a woman alive. I spoke to her and begged her be patient as we would rescue her. Two men then dug down to pull her out.

Then another voice was heard and it came from underneath where we had been working. A man was buried beneath and rubbish was carefully dug away, we had to haul him out from under the pile of ruins. I begged the man to lay perfectly still and hoped we should soon release him. I attempted to move part of a plank that pressed against his leg. He was in agony and it was necessary to cut through some more timbers with a saw. Happily we succeeded and the people gradually drew him out, feet foremost. I had the enjoyment of helping to bear him on a shutter into the hands of the nurses. I had long been a labourer in the hands of God to save immortal souls, but here I was labouring to save bodies".

The general belief was that the fall of the wrought iron roof was due to the weight of the scenery attached to it being too great for the freshly built walls. The architect of the building was quick to respond to criticism and had a lengthy statement recorded in a Sunday newspaper. He stated that although some concern had been expressed over the safety of the roof some twenty four hours before the catastrophe, he had been kept in utter ignorance of the situation.

# Woeful End of a Whitechapel Washer Woman

One morning during the last week of December in 1836, a bricklayer discovered a human trunk near some new buildings in the Edgware Road, London. The find produced a strong sensation in the city and the police were soon actively engaged in attempts to throw light upon the matter. An inquest on the remains, which medical examination showed to be those of a female, returned a verdict of wilful murder against some person unknown.

The next significant step occurred when the Lock man of the 'Ben Jonson Lock' in Stepney Fields, found a human head jammed in the lock gates. Close examination proved that it belonged to the previously discovered trunk. This find was followed by the discovery in an osier bed near Cold Harbour Lane, Camberwell, of a bundle containing two human legs. These were missing members of the same mutilated trunk and there was sufficient evidence to establish conclusively that the woman, thus collected piecemeal, had been barbarously done to death.

Eventually, towards the end of March 1837, the police achieved a major breakthrough in the case. A man who asked to view the head identified it as that of his widowed sister, Hannah Brown, who had been missing since the previous Christmas Eve.

Immediately investigations began to ascertain where and with whom she had last been seen. This brought suspicion on a man named James Greenacre whom she was to have married. On the day Hannah Brown was last seen she had left her residence in a coach, in company with Greenacre. In her possession at the time was money and property to the value of £500. A warrant was at once issued for Greenacre's apprehension, and he was arrested within days at an address in Kennington. In his company at the time was a woman named Sarah Gale, and she was also arrested.

Greenacre, a stout man wrapped in a brown great coat, assumed an air of insolent bravado. On his being apprehended, he remarked to the officer, "You are but just in time; tomorrow I should have started for America". The fifty year old man's words rang true as in his pocket was a receipt for his passage money. His despair must have been great because after a day of interrogation he attempted to destroy himself by strangulation, being observed just in time.

As the evidence unfolded the suspicion against Greenacre grew to a certainty. Hannah Brown, a washer woman supposed to be worth some money, had realised all her effects and taken them, with her furniture, to Greenacre's lodgings. The two, when married, were to emigrate to Hudson's Bay. A neighbour of the woman observed that the couple had seemed "perfectly happy and sociable and eager for the wedding day".

When brought before the Magistrates, Greenacre asked if he may address them. The Magistrates agreed and, after the woman arrested with him was removed from the court, he spoke as follows:

"There has been a falsehood stated. I never had any words with Mrs. Brown, nor ever said I had. I understood she was a woman of property, but I found out that she was a very loose character. There was duplicity on both sides, for I represented myself as a man of property and although there are many coincident circumstances which may cost me my life, I'll speak the truth.

I had this female (meaning his fellow prisoner) lodging in a room, and she used to wash and cook for me; but on becoming acquainted with Mrs. Brown I told her to leave me, which she did.

Mrs. Brown came to my house on the Christmas Eve about seven o'clock, rather fresh, for she had been treating and drinking with some coachmen. She insisted on having some rum for tea, and we had some. I then thought it a good opportunity to press her for a statement of her circumstances, as she had repeatedly said she could at any time get £300, or £400. She declined answering my question, and I then told her that I had found out that she had been trying to obtain silk gowns in my name, but had been refused. She feigned a laugh, and retaliated by saying that I had misrepresented the state of my property.

During this conversation she was rocking herself backwards and forwards, when I put my foot against her chair, and she fell backwards, her head coming with great violence against a clump of wood; that alarmed me and I went round the table and took her by the hand, and kept shaking her, but she appeared to be dead. As regards my feelings, it is impossible for me to give a description, from the agitation I was in. I thought if I called any one in I should be put down as her murderer, so I unfortunately came to the determination which I did in manner as is already known to the world. I thought it might be the more safe way than if I gave an alarm of what had occurred. No other person had the least knowledge of what I have now stated. The female here I exonerate, for she was away at her lodgings in Carpenter's Buildings.

Some days after I had put away the body, I called on Sarah Gale and asked her to return to me, telling her that the woman I was to have been married to had left her trunks and things, and we will pledge them between us. The whole of them fetched £3.5s. The deceased had eleven sovereigns and three shillings, which I took from her".

While relating his story the prisoner appeared perfectly calm. He realised the hopelessness of his situation yet made every effort to exonerate Mrs. Gale from any blame. Suspicion still hung over the woman's role in the killing and consequently the pair of them were committed for trial.

This took place at the Old Bailey and in that court he admitted he was guilty

*A warrant was issued for the
arrest of James Greenacre*

*Sarah Gale was sentenced to penal
servitude for life*

of manslaughter. Once more Greenacre gave his evidence in a way that was aimed to deflect blame from Mrs. Gale. He spoke to the court of his method of disposal of the *corpus delicti*, relating how he had got rid of the head. This he had wrapped in a silk handkerchief and carried through the streets under his coat-flaps, and then onto a crowded city omnibus. Leaving the omnibus, he had walked along by the Regent's Canal, at which point he conceived the idea of throwing the head into the water. Another day elapsed, according to his confession, before he disposed the rest of the body.

His attempt to clear Mrs. Gale was not helped when it was adduced in evidence that Mrs. Gale had been at his lodgings the very day after the murder. She had been observed busily engaged in washing down the house with mop and bucket.

Greenacre's hope lay in the jury believing his statement that Hannah Brown's death had occurred in a somewhat accidental manner and that, in a state of terror, he had dismembered her body so that he may dispose of it. The inference was that Greenacre had lured the woman to his apartment for the sole purpose of taking her life.

According to the medical evidence, Hannah Brown had been alive when decapitation commenced.

The Old Bailey jury, without hesitation, brought in a verdict of wilful murder against the accused. The woman Gale was sentenced to penal servitude for life, and James Greenacre was sentenced to death.

The first Monday of May 1837 was the date set aside for his execution. It had been rumoured for sometime that Greenacre would be executed at Horsemonger Lane instead of Newgate gaol. Nonetheless, at an early hour of the morning, the Old Bailey and the space around the angles of Newgate were thronged with a clamorous multitude. There were people from every grade in society, although the greatest mass was of the lowest order.

Many hundreds had spent the night sleeping on the steps of the prison and St. Sepulchre's Church in order to procure a commanding site. Several people remained all night actually clinging to the lamp posts to ensure their vantage points.

The gathered populace did not spend their time reflecting on the ghastly crime, but spent the interval in jokes and amusements. Suspense concerning the place of execution was put at an end at three thirty in the morning when workmen appeared from the gates of the courtyard with boards for the erection of the gallows.

The clinking of the hammers, the ringing of the chains, and the concussion of the boards as they were incorporated in the platform was the signal for a great influx from every part of the metropolis.

By six o'clock the machinery of death was conspicuous at a great distance. The height of the horizontal beam of the gallows from the base of the platform was about twenty feet. Those who could not approach any nearer were glad to view it from Ludgate Hill, and the roofs of the houses were covered with spectators.

As the morning advanced, the multitude became consolidated in one vast aggregate, through which neither coaches, cabs or any kind of vehicle could make their way except with great difficulty. The police at once began to fix blocks and bars at the termination of the different avenues to prevent any fatal crushing among the gathered populace.

At eight o'clock on that Monday morning the bells tolled the hour of death and Greenacre, led by the chaplain, made his way to the gallows. All his fortitude had left him and he was unable to speak. His lips quivered as if he were vainly endeavouring to articulate the responses of the reverend gentleman who preceded him. One of the officers was obliged to support him or he would have fallen. He neither turned to the right nor the left, and his eyes were closed as he walked along the narrow passage which led from his prison cell to the platform.

On his appearance outside, Greenacre was greeted with a storm of terrific yells and hisses, mingled with groans, sneers and other expressions of reproach, revenge and hatred. He answered nothing to the last questions put to him, nor did he seem in any way moved – indeed, he could not have been more depressed by the hostile reception. He said not one word of hope, repentance or reconcilement; nor did he make the anticipated speech of self-vindication for posterity. He had always complained that his contemporaries, especially the press, had cruelly prejudiced him.

When the dreadful uproar had, in some degree, subsided, Greenacre bowed towards the chaplain and the sheriffs and seemed anxious to thank them, but he could not speak. At length he faintly uttered his last sentence with a final look of contempt at the crowd, saying, "Don't leave me long in the concourse". Scarcely had the last syllable fallen when the signal was given, the spring touched and Greenacre was dead without a struggle.

He had left no dying directions, save that his spectacles should be given to Sarah Gale. Due to the nature of the crime, much personal injustice was perhaps done to him. He was by no means an ugly man, he stood at least five feet eleven inches tall and his figure was erect and gentlemanly. His eyes were remarkably full, clear and penetrating. He was said to have been a scoffer at religion from his youth to his last days, and no criminal ever displayed greater mental consistency and fortitude. None ever needed it more, for he died an object of unmitigated horror and execration to all who had heard of his atrocious crime.

The concourse that thronged the Old Bailey and the space around St. Sepulchre's church could not have been less than twenty five thousand persons. Many stayed to gaze upon the hanging murderer until the executioner returned to remove the body from the place of execution.

# Murderers Of Muswell Hill

Early in the morning of the 14th of February, 1896, the residents of the Muswell Hill area of London were shocked to hear of the killing of Henry Smith, a retired engineer, who was 79 years old. Mr. Smith had resided for many years at a house called Muswell Lodge, in Tetherdown. He had lived quite alone, keeping no servants and attending to his own wants and cooking. He did, however, employ a gardener called Charles Webber who, besides his duties outside, didoccasionally assist with the housework.

The garden ran down to Coldfall Wood and each night, before he left, Webber would set the alarm gun which was attached to a trip wire that ran along the rear of the premises. Usually, by the time the gardener returned in the morning the front gate would be unlocked and Mr. Smith would be up and about.

So it was with surprise that on the morning in the middle of February, when Webber turned up for work, he found the gate locked. After opening it with his key, he knocked at the house door, but received no answer. He then went round to the back of the premises and at once noticed that some small shrubs had been taken from the sill of the kitchen window. The window was shut, but there were marks as if it had been prised open from the bottom. He then examined the alarm gun and found that the wire had been lifted off its supports.

Concerned as to the safety of his employer, Webber dashed to enlist the support of his neighbours and within minutes they had forced their way into the kitchen. On doing so, they found the body of Henry Smith lying on the floor. His legs had been bound together at the ankles and above the knees and his hands were bound to his side. Round his head was wrapped a table cloth, tied below the chin with string. The string was cut immediately and, underneath the tablecloth, it was found that the man's neck had been tied round with a duster and over his mouth was a rag used as a gag.

A doctor was soon at the scene and concluded that the man had been dead for about six hours and that death had been caused by a dozen wounds inflicted to the head. A search of the house showed that the deceased's bedroom had been ransacked, and a safe, which had contained £100 in gold and other property, had been emptied of its contents. The footprints of two men were noticed in the garden at the back of the house and it was felt that the intruders had fled over the fence at the bottom of the garden and gone into Coldfall Wood.

Investigations were soon underway and the police were informed that two men with criminal records had been seen in the area the day before the killing. The pair were Albert Milsom and Henry Fowler, both in their early thirties and employed as casual labourers. They were known to associate with each other and when the police went looking for them, they were both missing from their Kentish Town homes.

A bulls-eye lanternt had been found at the scene of the crime, and within days enquiries connected Albert Milsom with it. The lantern had belonged to a boy

*The home of the Muswell Hill victim*

named Henry Miller who lodged in the same house as Milsom. He had kept the lantern at home and it had gone missing from the dresser a couple of days before the killing. The boy recalled that Milsom had not slept at home on the night of the crime, arriving back at the lodging house at seven o'clock in the morning. That same day the lad had gone with Milsom to purchase clothes from a shop in the Harrow Road and Milson had paid for the clothes with gold.

Several weeks then passed before the two wanted men could be found, but despite fears that they had gone abroad, they were arrested in Bath. Whilst under remand Milson stated that Fowler was entirely responsible for the crime and that he had taken no part in either the murder or the robbery. Fowler's response to the claims made by Milson was to say that Milson had put his foot on the old man's neck to make sure he was dead.

The trial of the two labourers took place in the middle of May, 1896 at the Central Criminal Court, before Mr. Justice Hawkins. The evidence was considered over two days and by mid afternoon on the second day the Jury had retired to consider it's verdict. The Jury had left the courtroom for only a few minutes when a scene of great excitement occurred.

The two prisoners were seated in the dock surrounded by warders when Milsom was observed to smile and whisper something to one of them. Fowler, apparently noticing this, made a determined attempt to reach Milson with the object of attacking him. A fierce struggle then ensued between Fowler and the warders, and the prison officials needed the aid of a number of constables to calm the prisoner. At length, Fowler was overpowered and both prisoners were removed from the dock.

On the return of the Jury the accused men were returned to the dock surrounded by warders, and with Fowler being restrained with handcuffs. The Jury returned a verdict of 'Guilty' and both men, when asked to respond, claimed they were innocent of the murder. His Lordship then donned the black cap and pronounced sentence of death on both prisoners.

In the opening case of the May Sessions, Mr. Justice Hawkins had sentenced William Seaman, aged 46, to be executed after he was found guilty of murder. His victims were John Goodman Levy, a retired business man in his mid seventies and his housekeeper, Annie Sarah Gale. As a result, it was arranged that all three convicted men would be executed on Tuesday, 19th June, 1896.

Whilst confined in Newgate Gaol, Milsom was to some extent buoyed up by the hope of a reprieve, but the Home Secretary saw no reason to interfere in the course of justice. During the last week of their confinement the three men took farewell of their friends and prepared to pay the price for their crimes.

On the morning set for the executions, the prison bell began to toll at a quarter to nine o'clock and the procession to the scaffold was formed in good time. All three condemned men walked with firmness to the gallows and, when they were placed on the drop, Seaman stood between the Muswell Hill murderers. Exactly on the hour the executioner, James Billington, withdrew the bolt and the drop fell.

Prior to their deaths Milsom said he was innocent, Seaman stated he had nothing to say, and Fowler made no statement at all.

After hanging an hour, the bodies were cut down and an inquest was held at the Sessions House in the Old Bailey. The Jury, after being sworn in, were taken to view the bodies, which were laid out in black coffins in the execution shed. On their way the jurymen had to pass through the corridor in which were buried the bodies of persons previously executed in the gaol. It was noticed that men were already digging the grave which was to receive the bodies of the three latest culprits. The inquest was told that the executions had been carried out satisfactorily and the usual verdict was delivered. Later that day the bodies were placed in the freshly dug grave.

# A Fatal Lambeth Fireworks' Explosion

When one thinks of fireworks, thoughts immediately go to that November day in 1605 when a Catholic conspiracy was hatched to blow up James I and his parliament. Guy Fawkes was found in the cellar beneath the Palace of Westminster, ready to fire a store of explosives. Several of the conspirators were killed, and Fawkes and seven others were executed.

In true British tradition, on November the 5th each year, the event is commemorated with fireworks and bonfires throughout the land. Down the years the popularity increased and, as it did, the manufacturers of fireworks multiplied. Despite the fact that the law of the nineteenth century prohibited the manufacture of fireworks in common dwelling houses, the practice was commonplace.

Such a manufacturer was Ralph Fenwick who, in 1873, occupied part of a house in Broad Street, Lambeth. It was a six roomed building situated a few doors away from the old Lambeth Workhouse and close to the south-western railway arch. Fenwick occupied the ground floor where, unknown to his neighbours, he carried out his business of fireworks maker. The first floor was occupied by the Lewis family and the top attic and kitchen were rented out to a family called Woods.

In the week prior to the annual event, Fenwick and his wife Jessie were busy preparing their perilous wares for the bonfire night's entertainment. On the Tuesday morning when most of their work had been completed, disaster struck. Suddenly, without warning the residents of Broad Street were alerted to Mr. Fenwick's illegal activities by a terrific explosion. The blast was so great that the front parlour window of the house was blown out and the lifeless body of Ralph Fenwick was hurled into the street.

The devastating explosion cracked the walls, destroyed the ceiling and set fire to the house. The neighbours rushed to the spot from their dwellings and saw Fenwick's body lying in the roadway, entirely naked. Through the gaping hole in the front of the building the dead body of Mrs. Fenwick could be seen, lying against the wall.

The house was soon ablaze, with the flames rising high above the roof. At the windows of the top floor, the elderly Mrs. Woods could be seen with her two grandchildren, shrieking for help. Below them, at the first floor window, were Mrs. Lewis and her two children, crying for assistance. Nothing at that moment could be done for them.

The people in the street called loudly to them to jump from the windows into the many outstretched arms of willing bystanders. Alas, they seemed afraid to approach too near the window, because of the smoke and flames. In the next instant the whole interior of the house seemed to give way and fall in.

The fire engines arrived in due haste and quickly subdued the flames. When the fire officers entered the smouldering wreckage, they discovered, besides the

*Scene of the firework explosion in Lambeth (from The Illustrated London News)*

body of Jessie Fenwick, aged 32, the remains of Drusilla Lewis, aged 48 and her two children – Alice, aged 9 and Sarah, aged 3; and Phillis Wood, aged 72, and her two grandchildren – Anne, aged 5 and Alfred, aged 2. Spared from the disaster were the two fathers of the dead children – Lewis, a lighter man and Wood, a slater, who were out at their work when the explosion destroyed their families. By good fortune, the youngest child of the Lewis family had been in the kitchen when the disaster struck and had been able to escape through a window into the back yard.

As they sifted through the wreckage, the fire-brigade men discovered some firework cases; the remains of a small 10lb keg of gunpowder; the bottom of another keg upon which were the exploded remnants of a fizzing powder; a composition of sulphur, charcoal and steel filings; a press for making rockets; tubes and funnels for filling the cases; and a charred piece of wood to which were fastened nine movable figures, evidently representing the Oxford or Cambridge eight with their coxswain.

It was thought that the 44 year old Fenwick had been at work making fireworks when, by over compression or by a spark from the fire flying into the powder, the explosion occurred. As a result his clothes were burnt or torn off his body by the fiery blast.

The tragedy led to cries for the law to be more strictly enforced with regard to this dangerous practice.

# Catastrophe on The River Thames

On the first Tuesday of September, 1878, the country was bathed in sunshine and holiday-makers were bent on making the most of what remained of the summer. To this end some 700 people were tempted to take a day's excursion on the *Princess Alice*, one of the largest saloon steamers of the London Steamboat Company.

At about ten o'clock in the morning, the boat made its way from London, bound for Gravesend and Sheerness. The outward journey was a routine one for the vessel, which was packed with a preponderance of women and children. Indeed, all went well and after the vessel's customary stop, the return journey was embarked upon. The *Princess Alice* steadily made its way back along the quiet estuary with its happy and contented passengers.

It was followed closely by the *Duke of Teck*, another saloon steamer belonging

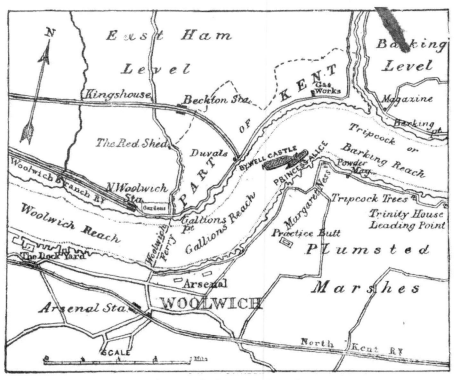

*Map showing the location of the disaster*

to the London Steamboat Company, which left Gravesend a few minutes after the departure of the *Princess Alice*.

Suddenly, the idyllic day on the River Thames was to turn to tragedy. Shortly after seven-thirty, within sight of the Royal Arsenal at Woolwich, the 158 ton paddle steamer was dramatically confronted by a large screw steamer, the collier *Bywell Castle*. The two steamers were in the middle of the stream, just off the well known City of London Gasworks at Beckton.

Within an instant the lofty bows of the *Bywell Castle* overshadowed the side of the saloon deck of the *Princess Alice*, grinding along the bulwarks and ploughing into her amidships, until the water rushed through her side and swept into the engine room. The *Bywell Castle* was six times the size of the pleasure craft and, with the momentum of her great mass, she cut through the *Princess Alice* like a knife through butter. The paddle steamer was mortally wounded. Her boiler exploded as the saloon section was lifted bodily from the deck and the vessel broke into two.

The passengers on board were filled with horror and a great rush was made to the aft of the vessel as the bow subsided and swiftly plunged beneath the water line. The vast bulk of her human freight were hopelessly engulfed in a gigantic trap.

The *Duke of Teck* steamed straight to the spot after witnessing the devastating collision. She found the water already covered with a tangled mass of wreckage, and was aided in her rescue attempt by a fleet of small boats which hurried from their vessels anchored nearby. Frantic attempts were made at rescue and ropes

*The idyllic day turned to tragedy for those on board the stricken 'Princess Alice'*

were thrown down from the *Bywell Castle*. The air was filled with fearful shrieks, and those on board the *Duke of Teck* succeeded in dragging several bodies, some dead and some alive, into their vessel.

That day there was a strong ebb tide and this hindered matters by carrying many of the passengers down stream and away from hope of rescue. The water was filled with drowning people, clinging to anything that floated and praying that rescue would soon be on hand. All that was humanly possible was done, but in the gathering gloom of the September evening the reality was that the majority had perished. Seamen toiled throughout the night and boats lay near the scene in the forlorn hope that additional souls might be saved from a watery grave.

At the first count, the engineer of the *Princess Alice* and some forty passengers were said to be saved, but the Captain, William Grinstead, and the majority of his crew were amongst the lost. On Roff's Wharf, the boardroom of the steamboat company was turned into a temporary mortuary and the gas was lit in the Town Hall to receive more of the dead. The floor of the boardroom was almost covered with the retrieved bodies, the corpses laid in order with identification labels on their breasts. The majority of the dead were wome,n and among the harrowing sight were the bodies of four children, mere babes, laid alongside each other on the balcony of a boardroom window.

With daybreak, the search was resumed and it continued all day. Hundreds of dead remained engulfed in the saloons of the buried wreck. Boats went to and fro above the spot, and at high water the only marks to indicate the spot where the *Princess Alice* went down, were the barges positioned to warn passing ships of the danger that lay hidden below.

*Relics of the dead exposed at Woolwich Dockyard (*Illustrated London News*)*

The *Bywell Castle* had been in the charge of an experienced pilot and he professed his utter inability to account for the fatality. Captain Harris, the ship's Master, stated that he stopped his engines as soon as he saw the danger and that he launched his rescue boat as quickly as possible after the collision. This, he remarked, was very nearly swamped by those who clambered into it, although eventually in the region of 40 people were saved by that means.

According to the Captain the blame lay with the *Princess Alice* which, he felt, should have kept on her course on the opposite tack. It was not a view shared by all and the final conclusion was that the incident was a tragedy of indecision and misunderstanding. Each had misunderstood the moves of the other, each was convinced that the other was at fault, and there was no satisfactory solution.

The reality of the situation was that it was, to that date, the blackest tragedy the River Thames had ever known. If only the rudder of either vessel had been turned in the opposite direction, a day's pleasure trip would not have ended in such despair.

The London Steamboat Company offices in Woolwich and London were besieged by anxious friends and weeping relatives. For days afterwards the muddy bottom of the river was dredged for the bodies of the drowned.

In all, not less than 650 men, women and children perished and the personal trauma that survivors had to endure was immense. The Pier Master at Woolwich lost his wife and eight children, and the superintendent of the steamboat company learnt that his wife, his mother and four of his children were amongst those that perished.

Many of those who did survive struggled to come to terms with the fact that others near and dear to them had become victims of the catastrophe. The merest turn of either helm would have permitted the two vessels to scrape past each other; alas, it was not to be.

*Saloon of the Princess Alice*

# The Chelsea Murderer
# Shows No Remorse

During the summer of 1870, two cold-blooded murders took place in Chelsea and left the people of the neighbourhood filled with horror. The victims were the Rev. Elias Huelin and his housekeeper, Ann Boss, who both lived at 15 Paulton's Square, Chelsea. The reverend gentleman was a native of Jersey and had nephews and nieces living there. Despite being 84 years old, the Rev. Huelin retained active habits of business, holding a good deal of property in the neighbourhood and also possessing a farm in Lincolnshire, at which his nephew resided.

It was the Rev. Heulin's custom to go down to his farm every summer, and in 1870 his annual visit was planned for early in May. Accordingly, when he was missing from his home from the ninth day of that month, it was assumed he had departed for Lincolnshire.

One of the London properties that the Reverend owned was 24 Wellington Square which, that summer, was unoccupied and in the course of repair. The Rev. Huelin had employed a man called Walter Miller to do the necessary works.

On the day he went missing the Rev. Heulin was seen entering the premises at around eleven o'clock. Shortly after noon of the same day, Walter Miller met Edward Payne outside the Admiral Keppel public house in Brompton Road. Miller asked the man, who was a casual labourer, if he would "lift a drain for him", a task which Payne agreed to undertake and for which he promptly went to borrow a pick and shovel.

Within half an hour he was back at the public house. After the two men had quenched their thirst with a pint of ale, they went to the Wellington Square premises. Acting on Miller's instructions, the labourer set to work, cutting a hole about 3 feet deep and 7 feet long in the yard. The hole was to extend to 3 feet under the wall of the water-closet. Payne suggested taking the floor of the closet up, but Miller remarked that "perhaps the old gentleman who was employing him would not like it". Whilst Payne was at his work, Miller lay down on a heap of ballast in the yard and remained there throughout.

When the job was done both men went into the back kitchen of the house. Miller told Payne that he had better leave his tools there, as he wanted him to return next morning to finish the drain, once the old gentleman had approved it. The following morning, when Payne returned to the house, he could not get in and subsequent visits also proved fruitless.

On the Wednesday evening a van proprietor and greengrocer, Henry Piper, who lived in Marlborough Road, Chelsea, was asked by a man with a French accent if he could remove some luggage from the Paulton Square address. On his arrival at the house Piper was shown downstairs and told that a box that lay under the dresser was for removal. Whilst he was cording the box, he felt something wet on his hand and, as he looked at it in the candlelight, he observed that it was blood. He also noticed a pool of blood beneath the box, and he immediately challenged the man who had employed him to explain the contents of the chest.

In the presence of a couple of women who were looking after the house, the 'Frenchman' then became angry and, dropping his accent, told Piper to, "Go back, you carman; do your work, and cord that box". The carter replied in the negative and told the man he did not intend to lose sight of him.

The 'Frenchman' reacted by putting on his coat and leaving the premises with Henry Piper in pursuit. When they reached the King's Road, the carter saw a constable standing under a lamp post and, approaching him, he told him of his concerns. At this point the 'Frenchman' attempted to flee, but Piper forestalled him and the pair of them returned to Paulton Square with the officer.

The box, when opened, was found to contain the body of Ann Boss, the housekeeper who had served the Rev. Huelin. The police officer had broken the box open with a poker and, on moving the body, it was seen that a length of cord was tied very tightly round the victim's neck and that strangulation had taken place. Blood had flowed from the mouth and nose and had run down the side of the box.

The bogus 'Frenchman' was taken into custody and it was soon revealed that he was, in fact, the 30 year old Walter Miller, who was a plasterer by trade. At the Chelsea police station he appeared depressed, weak and pale and would not speak.

In his possession was found a bottle which was empty, but smelled of laudanum. Fearing that he may have poisoned himself, the police surgeon gave him an emetic in coffee and brandy. The emetic acted, but there was no trace of poison in the result. Nonetheless, it was thought wise to remove him to St. George's Hospital, where he remained for a couple of days.

Meanwhile the police were concentrating their efforts on the disappearance of the Rev. Huelin, and by Thursday afternoon a search of the Wellington Square house was underway. In the back kitchen a pick, spade and shovel were found, and a battered and soiled hat was discovered under the sink. The inside of the hat was wet with blood. That night, digging took place in the garden until half past eight.

The following day the labourer Edward Payne was on hand to assist the officers and point out to them where had he dug the drain. At length the body of the Rev. Huelin was found, dressed in shirt, trousers, waistcoat and boots. Around the neck of the corpse was rope with a knot under the right ear. The rope was seen to be tight enough to have caused strangulation. In a cupboard under the stairs, marks of blood were found and it was believed that, prior to burial, the body had been stored in there.

The trial of Walter Miller took place in the middle of July, 1870 and there was great interest in the events of that week in May. Proceedings at the Central Criminal Court were under the directions of Lord Chief Justice Cockburn. The accused, a lithe looking man, of above average height, with light hair and fair complexion, pleaded 'Not Guilty'.

The evidence was entirely circumstantial but established a series of facts which directly connected the prisoner with both murders. Yet doubts existed because a char woman, named Middleton, and her daughter, who had been employed by Miller to look after the Paulton Square premises, testified that the 'Frenchman' and the accused were not the same person. The 'Frenchman' had been about the house with Mrs. Middleton and searched for papers, and yet she claimed that she had never connected the two.

In the guise of the 'Frenchman', the accused had represented himself as Mr. Huelin's nephew, with the intent of claiming his possessions. Speaking in broken English, he had been eager to lay his hands on documents belonging to his uncle and when one lady turned up to pay the Rev. Huelin her rent, he stated that he had the authority to take it.

The fact that Walter Miller had been apprehended after posing as the 'Frenchman', banished any doubt in the jurors' minds, and, after a two day trial, they took just ten minutes to find him guilty. After a brief pause the Lord Chief Justice assumed the black cap and proceeded to pass sentence of death on the prisoner. He told Miller that he had deliberately killed two people for the sordid and miserable purpose of getting possession of the Rev. Huelin's property and that he had gone, whilst still reeking with the blood of one victim, to take away the life of another. His Lordship then urged him to repent of the wickedness he had done and concluded by saying, "May the Lord have mercy upon your soul".

The Lord Chief Justice then called up the witness Henry Piper and told him that it was mainly owing to his determination and courage that Miller had been brought to justice. He then informed him that an Act of Parliament enabled him to mark his sense of conduct and reward him with the sum of £50. The announcement elicited a cheer in the gallery, which was promptly suppressed.

The execution of Miller was arranged for the first day in August, within the precincts of the Newgate Gaol. During the fortnight between sentence and his final day, the condemned man was visited by those relatives that resided in London. His wife, by whom he had two children, saw him a couple of times. Four days before his execution she gave birth to a third child. At the urgent request of the convict the baby was brought to Newgate by a nurse, in order that he might have the sad satisfaction of seeing it.

The officers of the gaol were fearful that the prisoner might seek to avoid his sentence by the commission of suicide. Consequently, a strict watch was kept over him. This surmise seemed to have some foundation because on the morning of his execution, as he was about to be pinioned, eluding for a moment the vigilance of his keepers, he ran head foremost against a wall of the cell, inflicting a wound upon the forehead. His reckless action stunned him for a while and for some time afterwards he lay on a mattress on the floor of the cell.

When the time arrived he refused to submit himself to the executioner and was pinioned in his prostrate condition. Declining to walk to the scaffold, Miller was carried on a chair by four warders. The executioner then completed the preparations and, with Miller still seated, the drop fell. After a brief struggle,

*The condemned cell in Newgate Gaol awaited Walter Miller*

during which there was more writhing than usual, he ceased to exist.

The black flag was then hoisted on the roof of the prison to denote that the capital sentence had been carried out. A considerable crowd had gathered outside the gaol, but there was no disorder and, on seeing the flag, the people quietly dispersed.

Towards evening, the body of Miller was buried within the precincts of the prison in conformity with the terms of the sentence.

# On a Foggy February Night
# in Greenwich

In the year 1818, among the residents of London Street, Greenwich, was a retired business man, George Bird. He was 83 years old and lived a lonely existence, relying on his lone servant, Mary Simmons, aged 50, to take care of his needs and regular habits.

Around mid-day on Sunday the 8th of February a brother of Mr. Bird paid one of his customary visits to the London Street address. Finding the premises apparently locked and receiving no reply to his call, he went to the house of a neighbour to enquire if he knew of his brother's whereabouts.

Fearing that something was amiss, the two men went round the back of the house in an attempt to solve the mystery. There they found all the doors and shutters fastened and returning to the front door, they attempted to gain entry by picking the lock. Alas, the key was on the inside and their efforts were thwarted. Becoming more anxious by the minute, they returned to the rear of the premises and gained entry by forcing the shutters of the kitchen window.

Once inside the dimly lit house they were confronted with a most harrowing scene. Entering a passage that led to the hall, they saw the body of Mary Simmons lying on the floor with her head towards the stairs. Stepping over the body they moved towards the parlour and there, laying dead on his back, was George Bird. Close by the old gentleman's body there was a candlestick and a broken candle, and alongside those lay the dead man's spectacles. His pockets were all unbuttoned and empty, and his watch was missing from his waistcoat pocket.

Alarmed at the dreadful scene, the men quickly checked the rest of the house. In Mr. Bird's bedroom a double chest of drawers gave all the appearance of having been ransacked, with each drawer half open and the contents tossed about. The bed was made and turned down at one corner, as if ready for sleeping in. On it were a couple of keys and a number of marks of blood. In the kitchen there was the servant's needlework and the table cloth was placed as if ready for supper. A few roasted potatoes and a tea-kettle full of water suggested supper had been in preparation.

Without hesitation the alarm was raised and Greenwich surgeon Frederick Finch was summoned to the scene. He observed that Mr. Bird appeared to have been slaughtered in a shocking manner. A couple of deep indentations on the forehead, and a long fracture on the back of the head suggested that several blows had been inflicted by a hammer with a sharp cutting edge and smooth face.

Mary Simmons had also suffered blows to the head from the same instrument and in all she had eight or nine fatal wounds. The jugular vein had been wounded, causing vomiting and her body appeared to have been dragged along the passageway and was lying in a pool of blood.

At once investigations got under way to identify the perpetrators of the terrible crime that appalled the residents of Greenwich. It was agreed that the killings had taken place the night before, just prior to Mr. Bird sitting down to his customary supper at 9 o'clock.

The night had been very foggy and a local woman recalled seeing a man at the door of Mr. Bird's residence, at around twenty minutes past eight. She had observed the man talking to the housekeeper and seen Mr. Bird making his way to the door. Some ninety minutes later, when she passed the house again, the shutters were closed and all seemed still. The man's back had been towards her and all she could observe was that his clothing had appeared dark.

A number of weeks were spent in enquiries, and it was only towards the end of March that events began to unravel the mystery. The solution evolved around a trunk which had been left with a Deptford couple for safe keeping. They were related to a man named Charles Hussey who, at the time of the killings, was lodging at a public house called the 'Tiger's Head', which was directly opposite Mr. Bird's residence in London Street.

He had left the trunk with the couple and when curiosity finally overtook them, they undid the cords that bound it and found inside two shirts, two sheets, a soup ladle, a silver wine strainer, a pair of gaiters and a ticket with the name of Charles Hussey upon it. The gaiters appeared to have marks of blood and vomit upon them.

A constable from Greenwich was the next to observe the contents of the trunk, and he identified the shirts, sheets and the silver as being property stolen from Mr. Bird's premises.,

Once the information had been relayed a search went out for the apprehension of Charles Hussey and on April Fools Day he was arrested. In his possession were found Mr. Bird's missing watch and a pocket book which had also been the property of the deceased. While taking off his boots during a thorough search, a ring was seen to drop to the floor. This, like the other items, was identified as having belonged to the unfortunate Mr. Bird.

The evidence was gradually building up against Hussey and at the end of July 1818, he stood trial at Maidstone for feloniously killing George Bird and Mary Simmons at Greenwich. The court was filled at half past seven in the morning and the trial began at eleven o'clock. When asked to plead, Hussey, a man of mild and placid countenance, stated in an audible and firm tone that he was not guilty.

The prosecution case was based on circumstantial, rather than direct evidence, although the amount of it was overwhelming. Hussey claimed that he had taken up a bundle that he had seen a man throw away and that was how the stolen property had ended up in his possession.

Various witnesses called gave little credence to Hussey's claim that he spent the evening of the murders in local drinking houses. The landlady of the 'Tiger's Head', where he was lodging, said she did not see Hussey that night until about ten o'clock.

The trial was a traumatic one for the Husseys with the accused man's sister and brothers being called to give evidence. So overpowered by their feelings, they could neither look towards their brother or the court. Indeed, his sister, Elizabeth Godwin, who had been custodian of the trunk prior to its removal to Deptford, was particularly overwhelmed and wept bitterly.

In all, some two hours were spent in summing up the proceedings, but after just a few moments consultation, the jury returned a guilty verdict.

When asked if he had anything to say before sentence of death was passed, Hussey repeated his claim that he was innocent of the murders. The Judge responded by pronouncing the awful sentence of death and informing the prisoner that no mercy could be extended to him.

Hussey had maintained his composure and firmness of nerve during the whole trial, and at the conclusion of the sentence he cast an anxious, agonising look towards the Judge. Without uttering another word, he was led away to prepare for his execution on the following Monday morning.

During the couple of days that Charles Hussey had before his date with the executioner, he was attended by the Rev. James Rudge. Despite the reverend gentleman's pleas the condemned man was reluctant to admit his guilt and in the presence of the gaoler he spoke the following words.

"What good will it do for me to disclose anything I know of this murder, now I am going to suffer for it. The secret had better die with me. You must not press me further, I am innocent of it".

On the morning of the execution the Rev. Rudge had arranged to visit him at an early hour to administer the sacrament of the Lord's Supper. When the two men were alone Hussey told the minister that he had spent a troubled final night, being unable to compose himself to rest.

The Rev. Rudge implored him to unburden his soul by making a frank confession of the events on that foggy February evening. Charles Hussey had begun to take comfort in his counsellor's ministering and at once began to divulge the secrets he had resolved would die with him.

He began by stating that he was not the murderer, but planned and instigated the robbery. He had made the acquaintance of two men, who he named, and after learning that Mr. Bird was very rich proposed the robbery. One evening, while drinking in the 'Tiger's Head', he, and one of the men, had observed Mr. Bird sitting in one of his rooms at a table whereon was a good deal of gold and a number of what appeared to be bank notes.

A couple of earlier attempts at the robbery were aborted and then on the foggy night they resolved to carry out their plan. Hussey stated that he was given the job of look-out while the other two men entered the premises and attended to the elderly gentleman and his servant.

When he was admitted to the premises he claimed that he was alarmed to find the pair had been brutally slaughtered. His accomplices claiming that it could not be helped due to the resolute resistance of the servant and the old man.

All three men then left the house within a few minutes and went into the park. There, by the light from a dark lantern, they began to divide the property, which was tied up in a sheet.

He claimed that in the bureau a great many guineas had been found and that the other two resolved that they should share them and he should have the bank notes, watches and other silverware.

After the dividing of the spoils he stated that the three men went their separate ways and that he only saw the other two on one further occasion. Hussey claimed that at the time of the murders the two accomplices had been about to sail for the East Indies, and that some four or five days afterwards he had learnt that the ship had gone.

His final confession complete, Charles Hussey was taken to the gallows and subjected to the extreme penalty of the Law. The last ditch confession, whilst not saving his life, had posed the question as to the possibility of the greater share of the guilt being on the shoulders of two other men.

# On the Trail of the London Body-snatchers

It was common practice during the first thirty years of the nineteenth century for surgeons to receive exhumed bodies with the intention of dissecting them. In their quest for improving medical knowledge surgeons resorted to buying the corpses, and thus grew a gruesome trade in grave robbing.

The situation was highlighted in the autumn of 1831, when the authorities became aware of two notorious body-snatchers, John Bishop and Thomas Williams. Their activities came to light following a visit by the pair to the dissecting room at the King's College, on the first Saturday in November in that year.

Just before noon on that day John Bishop, accompanied by a man named James May, rang the door bell of the establishment and received the attention of the porter, William Hill. The porter was familiar with them from previous visits. When asked what their business was, they replied by asking if the College was interested in a male subject, aged 14, in exchange for 12 guineas.

The porter told them that he could not give that price for they did not particularly want any bodies at that time. He then said that if they waited he would acquaint Richard Partridge, the demonstrator of anatomy, with the matter.

Eventually the visitors and Mr. Partridge came to an agreement for the payment of 9 guineas in exchange for the body, Bishop and May agreeing to return with their merchandise within the hour. The pair kept their word and, along with Thomas Williams and another man called James Shield, who was enlisted to aid in the transporting of the corpse, they arrived at the dissecting room carrying a hamper.

When the hamper was opened it was seen to contain a sack in which the body was stored. May, who appeared to be somewhat tipsy, then turned the body rather carelessly out of the sack. The porter, perceiving that the body was particularly fresh, then asked for cause of death. Bishop replied that he did not know and stating that it was no business of any of them.

Hill, who was experienced in these matters, observed that the appearance was different from that of a body that had been laid in a coffin. The left arm was turned up towards the head, with the fingers of the hand being firmly clenched. Significantly, there was no sawdust about the hair. The men were then asked to wait in an adjoining room whilst the porter showed the corpse to Mr. Partridge. During the next few minutes several gentlemen connected with the College viewed the body and, along with Mr. Partridge, they became suspicious. Richard Partridge's suspicions were aroused by the swollen state of the face, bloodshot eyes, swollen lips, a cut over the left temple, the rigidity of the limbs and the freshness of the body.

Mr. Partridge then entered the room where the men were waiting and, showing them a £50 note, he told them he must go and get it changed in order to pay them.

However, instead of seeking change, he went to the police and within a short time the four men were taken into custody.

When the men arrived at the station house in Covent Garden, they all appeared to be labouring under the influence of drink. The police officers quizzed the men with regard to how they had obtained the body. When Bishop was asked what his occupation was, he replied to one of the officers, "I am a bloody body-snatcher".

The corpse was also taken to the station house and it was observed that the teeth had been extracted. It was to be later revealed that May had, on the previous day, visited a dentist in Newington Causeway and offered for sale a set of teeth. He had asked for a guinea, but the dentist agreed to pay only 12 shillings, due to the fact that one of the teeth was chipped and because he suspected they were not all from the same mouth. May's response to this was, "Upon my soul to God, they all belonged to one head not long since, and the body has never been buried".

Early investigations also brought to light the fact that on the Friday evening, at seven o'clock, both May and Bishop had visited the dissecting room at Guy's Hospital. May had carried the body in a sack and when the porter at Guy's Hospital declined to purchase the corpse, the pair had requested that they leave the body at the hospital over night. The four of them visited the hospital the next day to collect the sack and its contents.

There was little doubt that the suspects were involved in illegal activities, but it was a few days before the police were able to be reasonably positive about the victim's identity. The evidence eventually pointed to an Italian boy called Carlo Ferrari who had lived in England a couple of years. He had been well known in the Oxford Street area, often having a squirrel type cage containing two white mice, strung around his neck.

Bishop and Williams lodged in a couple of cottages in Nova Scotia Gardens, and a fortnight after their arrest two police officers minutely searched Bishop's residence. They probed the garden areas with an iron rod and when the rod met with resistance, they began digging. Soon they had unearthed a jacket, a pair of trousers and a small shirt. In another patch of the garden they discovered a blue coat, a striped waistcoat and a pair of braces. The waistcoat had stains of blood on the collar and the shoulders. The articles had been buried about a foot underneath the surface and were covered with cinders and ashes.

It was soon apparent that Shields had been employed merely to assist in the transporting of the body and he was subsequently eliminated from the serious charges being developed against the other three men.

At that time there was a noted house of call for body-snatchers in Smithfield. It was called the 'Fortunes of War', and the three men were all traced to that public house on the day prior to their arrest. They had been in and out of the place throughout the day and May had been seen with a number of human teeth wrapped in a handkerchief.

By the first Friday of December enough evidence had been gathered to commence the trial of Bishop, Williams and May at the Old Bailey. They were charged with the 'Wilful Murder' of Carlo Ferrari and the 'Wilful Murder' of another person whose name was unknown. Besides those called to give evidence relative to the attempt to sell the corpse of Carlo Ferrari, a surgeon was called and he declared that the victim had not died from natural causes. The jury was also informed of the discovery of the two sets of clothes in the garden of Bishop's lodgings.

Amongst the witnesses was a six-year-old boy, Edward Ward, who lived with his father near the Nova Scotia cottages. He told the court that early in November he had gone to play with Bishop's three children and they had a new toy which was a cage containing two white mice. After the stream of prosecution witnesses the prisoners were called upon for their defence.

In his defence Bishop stated that he was 33 years old and had followed the occupation of carrier until the last five years, during which time he had earned his livelihood by supplying surgeons with subjects. He then solemnly declared that he had never disposed of any body that had not died a natural death.

With respect to the clothes found in his garden, he claimed that he knew nothing – stating that those areas had open access to all the neighbourhood's residents. He then asked the jury to remove all undue prejudices from their minds and, in conclusion, he stated that neither Williams nor May knew how he had obtained the body. Earlier in the proceedings Bishop had claimed that he had dug the body out of a grave and that he did not wish to implicate the watchmen of the graveyard who had trusted him.

William's defence was a brief one with him simply stating that he had never been engaged in the calling of the body-snatchers; and had only, by accident, accompanied Bishop on the occasion of the sale of the Italian boy's body.

May, in his defence, admitted that for some six years he had followed the occupation of supplying the medical schools with anatomical subjects; but disclaimed ever having anything to do with the sale of bodies which had not died a natural death. He went on to claim that he had accidentally met Bishop at the 'Fortunes of War' public house on the Friday on which the body was taken for sale to Guy's Hospital.

A cap similar in description to the one the Italian boy wore had been found in Bishop's home, and a woman from Hoxton Old Town was called to say that she had sold it to Bishop's wife two years previous, from her second hand clothes shop. However, the description that she gave of the cap she claimed to have sold did not match that of the Italian boy's cap and served little purpose in Bishop's defence.

On searching May's lodgings near the New Kent Road, the police had found a pair of bloodstained breeches and two women of dubious character appeared in court on his behalf. They stated that the blood on his clothes had been wholly due to an accident with a jackdaw a few days prior to his arrest.

Chief Justice Tindal then began to sum up the evidence, telling the jury that it was by no means necessary to know the names of the murdered parties. He pointed out that witnesses had placed the Italian boy close to the premises of Bishop on the night when the killing probably took place. In addition, a scuffle was heard that night in Bishop's lodgings and that the voice of Williams had been clearly heard whilst the disturbance was in progress. He then stressed that the evidence to show May participated in the killings was not decisive, and told the jury that it was up to them to determine to what degree he was involved.

The jury retired at eight o'clock that night and returned after an interval of thirty minutes. Every eye was fixed upon the prisoners as they once more entered the dock. Bishop advanced to the bar with a heavy step and he had the appearance of a man who had been labouring under the most intense mental agony. Williams came forward with a short, quick step and his whole manner suggested a feverish anxiety, which had not been apparent during the trial. May, who appeared very pale, had a firmer step than his fellow prisoners, but his look was that of a man who thought that all chance of life was lost.

The jury, when asked for their verdict, declared that all three men were severally 'Guilty of murder'. The verdict was received in court with becoming silence, but in a moment it was conveyed to the immense multitude gathered outside and they expressed their satisfaction at the result by loud and continued cheering and clapping of hands.

To such an extent was this expression of the popular feeling carried that the windows of the court were obliged to be closed so that the voice of the Recorder might be heard in passing sentence of death.

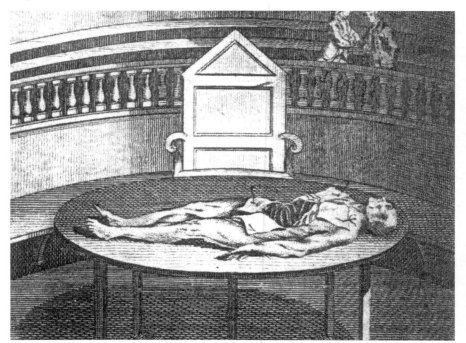

*The condemned men were set to end their days on the dissecting table,*
*as many before them*

The prisoners heard the sentence as they heard the verdict, without any visible alteration in their manner. When ordered to be removed, May raised his voice and in a firm tone said, "I am a murdered man, gentlemen, and that man", pointing to Bishop, "knows it". Bishop made no response, seeming to be engulfed by the awfulness of his situation.

The executions were set for the following Monday morning, outside Newgate gaol, and great interest prevailed throughout the weekend. In the hours that remained every effort was made to extract the whole truth from the condemned men and eventually John Bishop made a confession.

In his statement he questioned the identity of the Italian boy, but openly admitted to taking the boy home and feeding him with bread and cheese, followed by a cup of rum containing laudanum. He then told how he had, along with Williams, taken the insensible child into the garden, and after tying a cord round his feet, lowered him into a well. As the boy was submerged head first in the water, they had watched as he struggled and the water bubbled until life was extinct.

Bishop then went on to state that May had known nothing of the murder and that he himself had, along with Williams, been responsible for the murder of a young woman called Fanny Pigburn early in October. In view of Bishop's confession, the authorities decided to respite the sentence of execution on May and replace it with detention during His Majesty's pleasure.

The crowds began gathering on the Sunday in preparation for the executions, and when one of the three chains was removed from the gallows a general cry of, "May is respited" was uttered. The news did not excite much surprise, although a few individuals expressed their disapproval by yelling and hooting.

That Sunday evening the crowds increased and by midnight great numbers were assembled and windows that gave a view of the gallows were on offer for ten guineas.

Both prisoners rose at six o'clock on the Monday morning and appeared fervent in their devotions. By the time of execution, over thirty thousand spectators were gathered and, as the drop fell, the crowd gave a shout of exultation that was prolonged for several minutes.

After the bodies had hung for an hour, they were cut down and placed in a cart. The cart then moved at a slow pace through the crowds, the bodies being taken to a local house where an incision was made in their chests in the presence of the Sheriffs. That night the bodies were delivered for dissection, Bishop's to King's College and Williams to St. Bartholomew's.

## Postscript

In 1832 the Anatomy Act was passed making it an offence to rob a grave. The only corpses that it was permitted to use for dissection being those of people who had died in workhouses or hospitals and whose bodies were not claimed within seventy-two hours.

# A Cruel Captain and the Cabin Boy

Life at sea was harsh and cruel for the sailors of the early 19th century. Many vessels were engaged in warfare and others sailed the oceans to plunder the treasures of the world. The sailors were poorly fed, forced to live in cramped conditions, often brutally treated and gained little financial reward for their service.

Often a large number of those on a vessel had been forced aboard by the press-gangs who toured the ports to ensnare young and old alike. The press-gangs were the terror of wives and mothers, luring the unsuspecting men folk into accepting the King's shilling. Often the youths and men of London were too frightened to step out on the pavement for fear of the gangs. Whether in service to the King's navy or to the merchant fleet, the sailors commanded little respect from the officers and cruelty was commonplace.

Occasionally an account would emerge from the world's oceans that would highlight the plight of the men and boys at the mercy of the rulers of the waves. Such a tale of cruelty came to light in the summer of 1809, concerning a voyage that had taken place the previous autumn.

The case involved the death of a thirteen-year-old boy named William Richardson, who had died in the middle of November, 1808 on board a British transport ship called *Friends*. The captain of the vessel was John Sutherland and he appeared before the Admiralty Sessions at the Old Bailey in June, 1809, accused of the wilful murder of the boy whilst the ship was in the River Tagus, about a mile from Lisbon.

Crucial to the case was the testimony of a negro mariner, John Thompson who was examined by the Attorney General. He had been a seaman on board the *Friends*, having been left on duty on the 5th of November when most of the crew and officers had been granted shore leave.

That evening the captain directed the cabin boy, William Richardson, to attend him in his quarters. A few minutes later Thompson heard the boy cry out loudly, but he did not desert his lookout duties to see what was the matter because he supposed the captain was only beating the boy, as he often did. Only when the cries persisted did Thompson respond and when he entered the captain's cabin he saw Sutherland waving a dagger to an fro as he stood over the boy.

The boy was lying on the floor and, looking towards Thompson he cried, "Captain Sutherland has stabbed me". Lifting up his shirt, he showed a nasty gash on the left side of his stomach. The wound was a serious one and the captain acknowledged his actions by saying to Thompson, "I know I have done wrong".

On the instructions of the captain a nearby vessel, *Elizabeth*, was alerted, in the hope of enlisting medical aid. The boy was eventually attended to and his wounds dressed. The following morning the boy was transferred to the vessel *Audacious* where, despite tender nursing, he died some nine days later.

*Captain Sutherland attacked the cabin boy*

Amongst other testimony presented to the hearing was a statement made by William Richardson before his death. In it he claimed that Captain Sutherland had stabbed him twice in the belly. A surgeon from the *Audacious* was called to relate the details of the wounds inflicted on the boy and to confirm that they had led to his death. The surgeon was also asked his opinion of Captain Sutherland's behaviour after the stabbing, and he stated that the captain had been in a state of fever from agitation of mind.

Towards the end of the proceedings at least eight witnesses spoke on behalf of 40-year-old Captain Sutherland. Generally, they stated that he was a humane, good natured man, who was a good husband and a proud father of five children.

Despite the pleas for compassion the jury were unswerving in delivering a 'Guilty' verdict after a very short consultation. Sutherland was then addressed by Sir William Scott, President of the Admiralty, who told him to make the best use of the time left to him before he should be numbered with the dead. In a most feeling manner, he then told Sutherland that he was to be hanged on the following Monday at Execution Dock, and his body delivered to the surgeon for dissection.

On the last Monday morning of June, a few minutes after eight o'clock, the unhappy man was taken from his cell in Newgate gaol and placed in a cart.

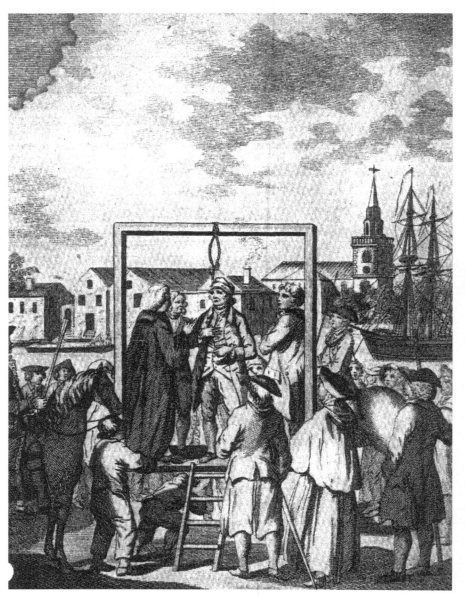

*Execution Dock at East Wapping was the venue for Captain Sutherland's haning.
He faced a similar fate to that of the pirate in this illustration, who was hanged
some years earlier*

Alongside him were the executioner and his deputy. The procession to the fatal spot was led by sixteen Sheriff's officers on horseback. The route followed was by Cornhill, Whitechapel and the Commercial Road, and during the whole journey the prisoner appeared to pray with the utmost devotion.

He then delivered his prayer book to the executioner and within seconds he was launched into eternity. His body was suspended for about half an hour, until the rising tide reached his feet. It was then cut down and delivered to the Surgeon's Hall for dissection.

# Park Lane Murder of Lord Russell

At about a quarter to seven on the first Wednesday in May, 1840 the neighbourhood of Norfolk Street, Park Lane, London, was thrown into a state of considerable excitement. One of the female domestics of Lord William Russell rushed out of his house calling for assistance. She had discovered his Lordship, with his throat cut almost from ear to ear.

The first person who entered the house was Emanuel Young, the butler of the gentleman who resided opposite his Lordship, whose attention had apparently been attracted by the shrieks of the female. Having ascertained that the statement was but too true, he immediately dispatched messengers for medical assistance.

A surgeon by the name of Henry Elsgood promptly attended, and he soon came to the conclusion that Lord Russell had been dead at least three or four hours. The Superintendent of Police and a considerable body of men were also soon in attendance, and they immediately set afoot an inquiry into the circumstances of his Lordship's death.

They were informed that the noble Lord, a seventy-three-year-old widower, had the previous day been in his usual good health and spirits. According to the butler, his Lordship had retired to his bed-chamber about thirty minutes after midnight and he had left him with a candle burning in a silver candlestick. The butler stated that he himself then retired and left his Lordship in the house with the valet and two female domestics who had gone to bed an hour previously.

One of the household servants had woken about half past six in the morning to attend to her domestic duties and when passing Lord Russell's bed-chamber, she had noticed his door was partially open. Struck with this unusual occurrence she looked into the room, thinking it probable that he had risen earlier than he was accustomed to. At first glance she observed Lord Russell lying in bed on his right side, apparently in a sound sleep. However, a close inspection revealed that the bedclothes were covered in blood and his Lordship's throat cut. It appeared that he had not struggled much, and that his death must have been instantaneous as the bedclothes were but little disturbed, and a portion of them was firmly grasped by his left hand.

The first impression was that he had fallen by his own hand, but this theory was soon dismissed as the most diligent search failed to uncover any instrument by which the fatal wound could have been inflicted. One of the maid servants, on going downstairs about seven o'clock, found that boxes and drawers in various rooms had been broken open and the contents plundered. It was also apparent that his Lordship's jewel box, which was on his dressing table, had been rifled of all its valuable contents, and it seemed that his gold watch, which he placed on the table every night, was also missing.

By six o'clock that night a coroner's inquest was held and the jury reached a verdict of 'Wilful Murder by some person or persons unknown'. The deceased Lord was the brother of the late Duke of Bedford and for many years he had represented the family borough of Tavistock in the House of Commons, subsequently becoming the minister at the Court of Lisbon.

Within hours the following circular was sent to the different station houses of the Metropolitan Police:

"C. Division. May 6, 1840
Found murdered in his bed, at 4, Norfolk street, Park-lane about a quarter-past seven o'clock this morning, Lord William Russell, with his throat cut. The following articles were stolen: one gold repeater watch, 'Lord William Russell' engraved inside; three gold seals attached with a ribbon, three plain gold rings, one set with turquoise, five silver table spoons, three silver dessert spoons, four large silver forks, two silver teaspoons – the crest, a goat".

Intense police activity and thorough investigations began to piece the mystery together. Firstly, it became clear that no forcible entry had been made and that marks on an outer back door had been made from the inside. Secondly, the police suspected that the intention of the crime was really murder, but it had been disguised as a burglary.

Consequently the police came to the conclusion that the crime had been committed by one of the inmates of the house. Suspicion at once fell on Francois Benjamin Courvoisier, the valet, a foreigner who had been in his Lordship's service for no more than three weeks. Courvoisier was at once taken into custody and the two female servants were placed under surveillance.

Apparently, the valet's strange demeanour had attracted attention from the first and he was said to have hung over the body in a state of dreadful agitation, answering no questions and taking no part in the proceedings.

A close search of the Butler's pantry, a couple of days after Courvoisier's apprehension, produced considerable evidence. Behind the skirting board, several of his Lordship's rings were discovered and nearby were found his Waterloo Medal and a ten pound note, which had gone missing from his note-case. Further searching uncovered the hiding places of a split gold key ring, a chased gold key and his Lordship's watch, concealed under the leads of the sink.

All this was evidence enough to warrant Courvoiser's committal for trial, but he still found friends and a liberal subscription was raised among the foreign servants in London to provide funds for his defence.

The young Swiss valet was 23 years old having arrived in London from Geneva, carrying out various menial tasks before serving his position with Lord William Russell.

Towards the end of June 1840, Courvoisier stood trial at the Central Criminal Court for the murder of his late master. The court was crowded to excess, the Duke of Sussex and a great number of the English and foreign nobility being present.

The court was informed of the discovery of the missing valuables in the pantry and the apparent lack of forced entry into the house. On the second day new evidence emerged when a woman told the court how Courvoisier had left a parcel with her. That parcel contained some of Lord Russell's stolen plates and immediately Courvoisier, who had pleaded 'Not Guilty', made a confession of his crime to his lawyers. They were placed in an embarrassing situation: to have thrown up their Brief would have secured Courvoisier's conviction. The lawyers went to the other extreme and, in an impassioned address, implored the members of the jury not to send an innocent man to the gallows.

Despite the plea, the jury without hesitation found Courvoisier 'Guilty' and he was left to the mercy of the Judge.

Before sentence was passed, his Lordship reminded Courvoisier of the age of his victim, his situation as his servant and the need to atone to society which had received a shock by such a crime. "It is fitting", he said, "that the crime committed in the darkness should be brought to light".

He then passed sentence of death in the usual manner, but he was dreadfully affected, so that at times his utterance was choked. Courvoisier was pale, but quite unmoved as he heard the sentence.

Once the verdict had been returned, it was generally reported that Courvoisier

*Francois Benjamin Courvosier had been in Lord Russell's service for only three weeks*

had made a full confession of his guilt. His motive was said to be a quarrel with his master, who had threatened to discharge him without a reference. According to Courvoisier, on the night of the murder Lord Russell had taken him to task over an act of forgetfulness. The murderer had then taken a carving knife from the dining room and, entering his master's room, had drawn the knife across his throat.

During the days that remained the condemned man made a number of statements, but they all varied considerably. Not much reliance could be placed on his confessions, therefore, although he was anxious to absolve the other members of the household from any blame.

In his final statement, the following words were recorded.

"The public now think I am a liar and they will not believe me when I say the truth".

The execution was set for Monday the 6th July, 1840 at Newgate gaol and on that day, as soon as the clock of St. Paul's had struck twelve midnight, the carpenters arrived in the prison yard and began with their preparation of barriers for the neighbouring streets. At two o'clock the apparatus of death was brought out into the prison yard and fixed in its proper place. The carpenters were occupied rather more than two hours in completing it. The sound of the hammers ceased as the bells of St. Sepulchre's chimed the quarter past four o'clock. The completion of the work was signalled on the part of the mob by a shout of triumph. The crowd at this time was by no means as large as had been expected.

Shortly after the carpenters began fixing the scaffolding, a body of sixty city police constables marched to the Old Bailey for the purpose of preserving order, and at a later hour in the morning sixty more arrived. The crowd did not increase much until six o'clock, when numbers began to arrive from all points of the metropolis. Long before the hour appointed for execution the whole line of view from Giltspur Street, Compter, down to Ludgate Hill presented one vast mass of human heads.

The general hum of conversation among the crowd, and the loud and heartless laugh which ever and anon struck the ear, would have induced anyone ignorant to the object which had called them together, to have supposed that they had come out on a holiday for the purpose of witnessing some passing pageant, rather than to behold a fellow creature sacrificed upon the scaffold.

The proportion of women in the crowd was small, and those who were present were mostly of the lowest and most abandoned rank of society. The windows of the houses commanding a view of the drop, however, presented a considerable number of well dressed women. The crowd, when at its greatest, probably numbered from 12,000 to 15,000 people, but it was admitted by all who remembered the occasion, that it never at any time equalled the numbers present at the execution of Greenacre.

From six o'clock many of the windows opposite the gallows began to be filled by persons who had engaged them. There were people at the 'Lamb' coffee house, at the 'George' public house, and at the undertakers premises next door.

Two hours before the appointed time the Rev. Mr. Carver, the Ordinary of Newgate, arrived at the prison and immediately proceeded to the cell of the wretched criminal, who he found in the act of writing. Courvoisier had retired to bed at eleven o'clock on the Sunday night, requesting the turnkeys, who sat up with him to call him at four o'clock next morning, as he had some letters to write.

During the night he had woken up just once, shortly after midnight, and the turnkeys had aroused him at the requested hour. He then spent the time, after dressing, in writing letters in the French language to his relatives, and completed these as the Rev. Carver arrived.

The next arrival in the cell was a Swiss clergyman and he, Courvoisier and the prison chaplain knelt together in prayer. By now the condemned man's form was much attenuated, and his eyes expressive of the deepest mental suffering; death was as visibly stamped on his features as it could have been on the death bed.

Shortly before eight o'clock, the signal for moving onwards was given. The bell tolled the knell of death as the mournful procession began to move, with Mr. Carver reading the burial service as he walked before the prisoner. The scene was of the most solemn character and, to many present, most deeply affecting.

The prisoner walked with a firm step to the drop. The moment he became visible to the mob a dreadful yell of execration was raised, which went to the hearts of all around him. Courvoisier himself, however, still stood firmly to the last.

The executioner, with the least possible delay, adjusted the rope round his neck and during this operation, which lasted about two minutes, the yelling and shouting were loud and incessant. The fatal bolt was then withdrawn and the drop fell. The hands of the murderer were slightly convulsed, and his legs very considerably drawn and bent upwards, until pulled down by the executioner from underneath, in order to shorten the victim's sufferings. He apparently died soon after the falling of the drop.

One of the letters written by the prisoner was to his sister and was dated "July 6th, 1840, Newgate, on the day of my execution".

# Ten-fold the Victims of a Newgate Day

On the second Wednesday of November, 1802 a body was discovered partially buried in a ditch, some 200 yards from the road upon Hounslow Heath. Investigations revealed that the corpse was a man called John Pole Steel who had resided at a house in Catherine Street, Strand. He had been missing since the previous Saturday. His battered body had been stripped of his hat, great coat and half boots, which he had worn on leaving home that evening.

The death of the gentleman on the road was added to that year's unsolved crimes, his mangled body being testimony to the cruel and vicious treatment handed out to him. All hopes of catching the perpetrators diminished as the local investigations failed to uncover any reliable evidence.

In fact, it was to be almost four years before the authorities were to receive any significant information about the crime. The revelations came to light after a court hearing in September, 1806 when a former coachman, called Handfield, was convicted of grand larceny in stealing a pair of shoes, and sentenced to transportation for seven years.

Whilst in the company of other convicted felons and on his way from Newgate gaol to board a hulk in Longston Harbour, near Portsmouth, he took part in a conversation about different robberies. His contribution was a reference to the unfortunate Mr. Steel and the fact that only three men knew anything about that murder. He had aroused the curiosity of his companions, but when they pressed him for more information, he remained silent.

A few days later, as he lay shackled in the transportation ship hulk, awaiting the long voyage across the high seas, he was visited by a Magistrate from Portsmouth. Word had filtered through to the authorities and when the official asked him if he knew anything about the Mr. Steel business, he answered that he did. He said that the events of that November night in 1802 lay heavily on his conscience, and that for the sake of public justice he would give evidence.

A police officer was immediately sent down to Longston Harbour to collect Handfield, and as they drove back to London, crossing Hounslow Heath, he pointed out to the officer the spot where Mr. Steel had met his death.

The questioning of Handfield led to the arrest of John Holloway, alias Oliver, and Owen Haggerty, two members of the labouring classes. Holloway was taken at the Brentford Election, and Haggerty was brought from on board the frigate *Shannon*, which was berthed at Portsmouth.

Handfield had been very detailed in his recollections of the crime in which he claimed to have played only a minor role. According to him, Holloway and Haggerty had approached him in the 'Black Horse' public house and told him of their intention to rob this particular gentleman who was sure to have property about him.

An afternoon of drinking was followed by a walk to the Heath and concealment in the bushes until Mr. Steel came along. When the gentleman was suddenly confronted by the three men who ordered him to "stop and deliver", he handed over his money. The men had hoped for a greater plunder than the few coins they received and Holloway and Haggerty began to turn out Mr. Steel's pockets. The gentleman had begged his assailants not to ill-treat him, but their agitation increased and Holloway, who had in his hand a large blackthorn stick, struck Mr. Steel about the head with it.

One blow led to another and soon the man was lying on the ground moaning and groaning. At this point Handfield claimed that he voiced his concern for their victim and told the others that he wanted no further part in the proceedings and was returning to London. Some distance down the road Handfield was overtaken by the other two who had been running to catch him. Holloway appeared somewhat irritable and informed him that the gentleman was cold and stiff and that they had 'done the trick'. On Holloway's head before the robbery had been an old soldier's hat, with ragged worsted binding, but now he wore the hat that the gentleman had been wearing. Handfield claimed that he told the others it had been a cruel piece of business and that he was sorry he had been a party to it.

Shortly after midnight the three men were in the 'Black Horse', in Dyott Street. A half a pint of gin was consumed as Holloway informed Handfield that, as he had not shared in the final danger, he had no right to share the spoils.

When the men met up a couple of days later Holloway was still sporting the victim's hat and only after Handfield had convinced him of the folly of wearing it did he agree to filling the hat, which had the name Steel in the lining, with stones, and sinking it in the Thames off Westminster Bridge. According to Handfield that was the last time the three men were together. For four years he kept the silence of thieves.

Not surprisingly both Holloway and Haggerty were stunned by their arrest and both denied any involvement. For seven days the pair were quizzed by the Magistrates, but there was no direct or strong circumstantial proof to corroborate the testimony of Handfield.

In the hope that, given the opportunity, the two men might condemn themselves from their own mouths, the Magistrates devised a devious plan. After each day's questioning the pair were placed in adjacent rooms, separated by a wooden partition with glass panels at the top. Behind these rooms was a privy, also separated by a similar structure, in which an officer concealed himself with notebook and pencil. The two suspects were able to converse fairly audibly with each other and as they did, the officer scribbled down the relevant comments. The conversation was to be their downfall with the Magistrates being convinced of their part in the footpad robbery and murder.

The two men stood in the dock at the Old Bailey on Friday, 20th February, 1807, and although both prisoners denied their guilt, the jury only needed ten minutes to return a 'Guilty' verdict. The case had lasted from nine in the morning until seven in the evening. The Recorder pronounced upon both men the sentence of death on Monday next.

It was stated that Handfield had received His Majesty's pardon for the offence of which he had been convicted in order to render his testimony valid. The price of his freedom had been the conviction of his accomplices.

\* \* \* \* \* \*

In an adjoining court-room on that Friday in February, Elizabeth Godfrey was indicted for the wilful murder, on Christmas Day, 1806 of Richard Prince, a gentleman's coachman. A couple of nights before his death Richard Prince had been instrumental in having the woman arrested, following an incident in the lodging house where they both resided in the Mary-le-bone parish.

Elizabeth Godfrey had been entertaining a gentleman in her room and when her visitor complained that he had been robbed of 18 shillings, Richard Prince called in the watch. This led to the woman being detained overnight in the watch-house.

Upon her release she let her feelings towards Richard Prince be known to all who would listen and on Christmas Day afternoon she went to his room and tapped on the door. The confrontation that followed was an unpleasant one with the man allegedly hitting her and the woman retaliating by stabbing him in the face with a knife. The wound inflicted was in the region of the left eye and Richard Prince was conveyed to the Middlesex hospital in a critical condition. In the care of the surgeons he lingered for over three weeks before dying from his wounds.

The accused woman claimed that she had not had any intention to claim her victim's life. The jury, however, took little time to pronounce her guilty and the Recorder informed her that the penalty for her crime was execution on Monday morning. When she heard the verdict all her firmness disappeared and she appeared to border upon a state of frenzy.

\* \* \* \* \* \*

With three executions planned, the crowd that assembled on the morning of the 23rd of February, 1807 was of unparalleled proportions.

By eight o'clock not an inch of ground was unoccupied in view of the platform. The pressure of the crowd was such that before the malefactors appeared, numbers of people were crying out in vain to escape from it.

A few minutes before the appointed time, Holloway and Haggerty were led into the press yard where they had their arms pinioned with cords, in the company of several noblemen and persons of distinction. As soon as Holloway was pinioned he fell upon his knees and protested his innocence in the most solemn manner. Praying to God, he pleaded that he might be dealt with in the hereafter according to his innocence. He concluded his devotions by stating that he and his companion were both innocent of the crime imputed to them.

Haggerty, in his conduct, endeavoured to follow the example of Holloway. All his declarations were to the same effect, although he did not possess the firmness of resolution of his accomplice.

*St Sepculchre's church*

As the clock struck eight, Haggerty, a slight man, came on the platform, apparently much impressed with his situation. He took little notice of the surrounding multitude, but was very attentive to the executioner. Holloway arrived on the platform with a seemingly undaunted spirit, and after bowing to the right and to the left he addressed the mob. In a firm and loud tone of voice he shouted – "Innocent, Innocent, Gentlemen! No verdict, no verdict, by God, Innocent". At that moment the executioner proceeded to do his business and placed the cap over Holloway's head, to which ceremony he reluctantly submitted.

The female malefactor, Elizabeth Godfrey, was the last on to the platform, and the reverend gentleman who was in attendance seemed to afford her much consolation. She was dressed in white and her interesting figure and decent deportment excited much pity in the beholders. She appeared very tranquil and resigned to meeting her unhappy fate with great fortitude. After conviction she had never denied the justice of her sentence, but had continually declared that she had not possessed the remotest intention to murder her victim.

The ropes all being fixed, a signal was given by the clergyman and the drop of the platform was struck away. The woman was dead in a few moments but the men struggled much, particularly Holloway.

The executions had led to great agitation amongst the 40,000 people gathered, and throughout the time the three were on the scaffold there were continual cries of "Murder! Murder!"

As the culprits were launched into eternity, the crowd that had gathered in Green Arbour Lane, opposite the Debtors' door, became involved in their own fight for life.

Amongst that section of the crowd were a couple of pie-men who had been doing a brisk trade. Suddenly, as the crowd surged forward, one of their baskets was upturned and the melee that followed was to be a deathly one. The pressure of the mob was intense and those that fell were unlikely to rise again. The ones that ended up on the ground were trampled on and suffocated. It was shocking to behold as the large body of the crowd were embroiled in a convulsive struggle for life. They fought with the most savage fury and, in consequence, great confusion reigned.

After a few minutes that seemed like eternity, the pressure of the crowd eased and the full horror of the occurrence was revealed. As fast as the mob cleared away, those on the ground were picked up and placed on boards and in carts and conveyed to the nearby St. Bartholomew's hospital. In all twenty-seven bodies were laid out in the Elizabeth Ward of the hospital to be claimed by their friends.

A further fifteen men and two women were conveyed to the hospital with severe bruising, one of the wounded men died later that night.

Two victims of the crush had been taken to St. Sepulchre's Church and one to the 'Swan' public house, bringing the tally to 31 deaths. Amongst those that died were one of the pie-men, a hackney coachman, a butcher's lad and a West Indian youth. A mother had lost her babe at arms and a father had seen his son crushed to death.

A day when three were set to die had delivered ten-fold the number of victims.

# East End Misery and Mutilations

During a three month period towards the end of 1888 a series of murders and mutilations took place in the East End of London that not only terrified the residents of the area, but shocked the whole nation.

The killer struck first on the night of the 6th of August, 1888, and his victim was discovered the following morning, lying in a passageway of the George Yard Buildings in Commercial Street. The mutilated corpse was that of Martha Turner, who was in her mid thirties, and the body had received over thirty stabs and cuts.

On the previous evening she had been seen in the company of some soldiers that frequented the ale houses along the river in Limehouse. No doubt she had been touting for business and offering her services for a sixpence, to any man so desirous. A surgeon who examined the body came to the conclusion that whoever killed Martha Turner knew how and where to cut.

The second crime, attributed to the same killer, occurred at the end of August when Mary Ann Nicholls was found dead on the cobbles in Buck's Row, Whitechapel. The woman who was a well known prostitute in her early forties, had been seen the night before staggering drunkenly around the neighbourhood, wearing a bright new bonnet on her head. She had been hoping to attract the attention of a gentleman with a few pence to spare, in exchange for her favours.

Her remains were taken to the Whitechapel mortuary and the corpse was a shocking reminder of her killer's brutality. Reports stated that the knife used must have been a large one and that it had been jabbed into the deceased at the lower part of the abdomen and then twice drawn upwards with ferocity. The first cut had veered to the right, slitting up the groin and passing over the left hip and the second cut had gone straight upwards through the centre of the body to the breast bone. The conclusion was that only a maniac could have carried out such a dreadful deed.

Within a week the killer had struck again, his latest victim being Annie Chapman who was in her late forties and who walked the street to earn money to pay her nightly lodging fee. On this particular night she was penniless and, after being turned away from a doss house in Dorset Street, she was seen heading towards an alleyway at the back of Hanbury Street, a well known haunt for prostitutes and drunken people.

As dawn broke a cry of "Brutal Murder" was heard as Annie Chapman's mutilated remains were discovered in the back yard of one of the Hanbury Street buildings. The killer had slain his victim in a similar fashion to the previous ones, but on this occasion the murderer had performed a bizarre laying-out ceremony, by carefully arranging at the woman's feet a few copper coins and a pair of brass rings, which he had wrenched from her fingers.

Enquiries revealed that this third victim had, in fact, been the wife of a respected veterinary surgeon, who had died at Windsor some eighteen months

*Buck's Row, Whitechapel, where Mary Ann Nicholls was found dead*

previously. The woman had been separated from her spouse for a long time on account of her drinking habit. Nonetheless, prior to his death the man had sent Annie Chapman a weekly postal order for ten shillings.

It was felt that the murderer must have fled the scene covered in blood, and a woman, who kept a public house called the 'Prince Albert', revealed that early that morning a stranger had entered her bar and asked for half a pint of ale. He had seemed anxious to conceal his face, with his stiff brown hat drawn down over his eyes and the collar of his long dark coat turned upwards. The landlady noticed there were blood spots on the back of his hands and that his shirt appeared to be torn. As soon as he had drunk the ale, which he swallowed at a gulp, he left the ale house in apparent haste.

The atrocities were soon headline news throughout the nation, and a host of newspaper reporters arrived amid the squalor of the East End slums to glean the latest information on the crimes. The drama was intensified when the police issued details of a letter said to be from the killer, and addressed to the Central News Agency.

In it the writer stated, "I am down on whores and I shan't quit ripping them till I get buckled. Grand work the last job was. I gave the lady no time to squeal". It was signed "Jack the Ripper" and his chilling comments ended with a reminder that his knife was sharp and he was ready to go to work again.

Two days later his threat became reality when, within the space of one hour, two more fell victim to his deranged acts.

*Annie Chapman's mutilated remains were discovered at dawn*

The alarm was raised shortly after one o'clock in the morning on the 30th of September. At that time, in an alleyway off Berners Street, a street seller discovered the body of 45 year old Elizabeth Stride, the wife of a carpenter. She was well known in the Spitalfields area. Of Swedish origin, she had begun to drink heavily after the loss of her two children amid the wreckage of the *Princess Alice* steamer on the River Thames.

That evening the woman had been seen in the company of a stranger in one crowded thoroughfare after another and, just minutes before her death, she had been observed lingering outside a working man's club in Berners Street. Blood was still pouring from a gaping wound in her neck when she was found.

*Elizabeth Stride – her body was discovered in an alleyway off Berners Street*

Before another hour had passed on that Sunday morning, a second victim was discovered in nearby Mitre Square. This time the body was found by a police constable who was out patrolling the dimly-lit alleyways. The victim was Catherine Eddowes, another lady of the night, in her early forties. Only an hour before she had been released from Bishopgate Police Station, having spent several hours sobering up in a cell after being found in a drunken state earlier that evening. The slaying of Catherine Eddowes had been a bloody affair and it was believed that the killer had stopped to wash his hands in a public sink before he fled into the night.

Within hours the Central News Agency had received a postcard besmeared with blood and in the same handwriting as the earlier letter. The sender was clearly proud of his latest exploits, stating – "You will hear about Saucy Jack's work tomorrow. Double event this time. Number one squealed a bit; couldn't finish straight off".

People suspected of being the murderer were hounded in the streets and the police employed blood hounds in the hope of tracking down the killer. Just what kind of criminal was being sought was emphasised a few days later when Mr. Lusk, the head of the

*Catherine Eddowes – her slaying was a bloody affair*

Whitechapel Vigilance Committee, received a package through the post. In it was half a kidney taken from the body of Catherine Eddowes. An enclosed message, addressed to Mr. Lusk, informed him of the contents and stated that the other half of the organ had been fried and eaten by the sender.

Although the killings had been confined within a square mile of the East End, the whole of London was living in fear and the prostitutes of the City were an unenvied group. Mistrust fell upon all classes of person; the surgeon, the policeman, the nobleman and even the midwife were viewed with suspicious eyes.

More and more police and plain clothes men were drafted into the area as anxiety prevailed. As if waiting for the excitement to reach fever pitch, the killer delayed his next atrocity for five weeks.

Unlike the other victims, who were all middle aged, drink-sodden drabs and the wrecks of slum vice, the next victim was the highly attractive Marie Kelly. She was new to the profession and, at 24 years of age, she actually possessed an apartment of her own – an enviable situation amidst the overwhelming poverty of the district.

Her death was discovered on the second Friday of November when the landlord called at Marie Kelly's apartment to collect her rent. What he discovered at the Miller's Court apartment sent him, wild eyed and in hysterical fear, in search of a policeman.

The killer had obviously spent some time at his work because the whole body of the pregnant prostitute had been cut up. Her face had been slashed repeatedly, her throat cut from side to side and most of her organs had been removed. On the pillow, beside her head, lay her heart, and on a table were placed her kidneys

*Sympathy was felt for the prostitutes who walked the streets in fear*

and her severed breasts. Bits of flesh were even hung on picture hooks around the walls of the apartment. The scene of the horrible crime was described by a senior policeman as the most gruesome he had ever witnessed in his long career.

One of Marie Kelly's acquaintances gave the police information of what he had seen – "I saw Marie Kelly with a man at the corner of Thrawl Street at two o'clock in the morning. He looked about 35 years of age and was dark, with a dark moustache turned up at the ends. He wore a long dark coat and spats over buttoned boots. He also had a massive gold watch chain with a seal attached, and carried a parcel covered with American cloth" (a shiny black material).

Two other prostitutes informed the police that on the night of the murder they had been approached in Spitalfields by a man carrying a shiny black bag. When the women asked him what was in the bag he had replied, "Something the ladies don't like".

During the days that followed the police diligently searched every drinking den and doss-house in the East End, and three men were eventually arrested. None of them proved to be the elusive Ripper and they were all released from custody.

The killing of Marie Kelly brought to an end the sickening series of murders and mutilations that were carried out in the name of Jack the Ripper. Long after the final slaying he held London in a grip of terror and, despite intense invest-igations, he was set to elude his would be captors. Eventually the hue and cry died down, and the East End returned to normality amidst its squalor and poverty.

## Postscript

Although the killings ended over a hundred years ago, the identity of Jack the Ripper remains a mystery that fascinates generation after generation. One theory brought forward, fifty years after the murders, was that a former surgeon had been responsible. It was claimed that on his death bed in Buenos Aires he uttered the following explanation.

That he had been a brilliant surgeon in the West End of London who had become a recluse when his wife died. He had then focussed all his hopes on his aspiring son, who was a medical student of distinction. The boy had met Marie Kelly in a cabaret in the West End and his short affair with the woman had led to disease and death a few months later. The father had sworn revenge and night after night he had toured the West End seeking the whereabouts of the woman. Eventually he was to discover that her life on the stage had become one of life in the gutters of Whitechapel.

Beginning his search anew in that area, he accosted one woman after another in order to find Marie Kelly's address. To ensure that no one would know he was on the trail of the woman he then silenced the prostitutes, removing their organs to add to his collection, which was the finest in the world.

From his fifth victim he gleaned the information he desired, and on that November night he called at Miller's Court and his young victim received the full frenzy of his grief and loathing.

The theory of the revenge-seeking surgeon was treated with the same doubts and misgivings as a whole collection of theories that have been expressed since the slaughters stopped during that autumn in Victorian London.

# Suffering End for Soho Murderer

Charles Dickens campaigned vigorously during the middle of the nineteenth century for public executions to cease, and hangings to take place in the privacy of the prison grounds. He was particularly scathing in his dislike for the public executioner, William Calcraft, and, in one letter to *The Times*, he implored that Calcraft should be restrained in his unseemly briskness, vulgar humour, lurid language and brandy.

*Charles Dickens campaigned vigorously against public executions*

Most executions were carried out with little fuss, but occasionally the culprit was observed to suffer unduly upon the scaffold, and the scene would lead to renewed cries to banish the gruesome spectacle from the public gaze. One such occasion was the last day in March, 1856 when William Bousfield was placed upon the scaffold at Newgate gaol.

Bousfield had been convicted of the murder of his wife and their three children in Soho. He had cut his wife's throat and delivered several more terrible wounds with a chisel, which he had then used to kill his children. The dreadful acts appeared to have been committed without any motive, and after the killings Bousfield had walked into the Bow Street police station and confessed his crimes.

The only defence offered at his trial was that no person in his right mind could have committed such an act. The pleas of insanity fell on deaf ears and once a guilty verdict had been delivered, the law was left to take its course.

After he had been condemned to die, attempts were made to persuade Bousfield to reveal the reason for his terrible crime, but after saying a few words he would suddenly check himself and not a syllable more would escape his lips.

It was believed that jealousy was the primary cause of the dreadful tragedy and, in a letter written to his father, Bousfield accused his wife of having committed adultery. It appeared that one of the unfortunate children who died by his hand had informed him, a few days before the murders, that she had seen a young man kissing his wife in the cigar shop that she kept. The man's frequent appearance in the shop had greatly infuriated Bousfield and it was felt that this had very probably led to his insanely jealous action.

Bousfield entertained strong hopes that his life would be spared, and he attempted to convince the authorities of his unsound mind with a series of irrational actions. His behaviour in this respect was of so clumsy a character that he was reminded that such a course could not possibly benefit him. Eventually he appeared to be resigned to his fate and on the last Saturday afternoon of his life he was visited by two of his sisters. They were very much distressed, but the prisoner exhibited a great deal of indifference during their visit.

When the sisters had gone, Bousfield, who was seated on the edge of his bed quite close to the fireplace, suddenly rose from his seat and threw himself head foremost into the blazing coals. The attendant warder immediately rushed upon him and dragged him from the grate. Other assistance was soon at hand and Bousfield's clothes, which had set alight, were stripped from his body. His mouth and the lower part of his face had been severely burnt and the surgeon of the gaol was at once sent for.

All that could be done was to apply cooling lotions to the prisoner's face in order to relieve the pain. The surgeon declared that the injuries were not of a dangerous character, although Bousfield's face was much swollen. From that time the wretched man refused to speak or receive any food, exhibiting an utter prostration and helplessness. The only nourishment that he could be induced to swallow being a little milk.

On the Sunday morning attempts were made to induce him to listen to religious instruction, but his indifference led the chaplain to abandon his ministrations. That night he was encouraged to take a glass of wine and this he did with some difficulty.

At half past seven on the Monday morning, the Sheriff and other officials arrived at the prison and fifteen minutes later, along with the governor, they proceeded to the prisoner's cell. As they entered, the condemned man was seen sitting on a chair, supported by two men, in an entire state of prostration. The attendants, from time to time, wiping away the froth that kept constantly oozing from his mouth, but not a sound or word escaped him.

Shortly before eight o'clock, William Calcraft was introduced, and at once proceeded to pinion the arms of the prisoner. The surgeon was then called upon and restoratives were administered, but with no apparent affect. The officers who had been supporting Bousfield attempted to get him to stand on his feet, but his utter helplessness made it impossible. It was then evident that he must be carried and the two warders took hold of his legs and another carried him by his armpits. In that listless state, nearly doubled up, he was carried to the foot of the scaffold. All the while the chaplain was reading the burial service and the prison bell was ringing out.

Under the instructions of the executioner a high back chair was brought from the prison and Bousfield was placed in it and carried up on to the scaffold. Calcraft, who exhibited an unusual nervousness, lost not an instant in putting on the cap and adjusting the fatal noose. As soon as he had secured the rope to the chain suspended from the beam, he ran down the scaffold steps and, without any signal, withdrew the bolt.

The chair dropped from under the culprit and he became suspended, but within seconds he exhibited a convulsive strength and power, to the astonishment of all. His shoulders and arms were raised upwards, his legs being thrown forward to gain a foothold on the platform. He then maintained that position until one of the officials went upon the scaffold and pushed down the legs.

Calcraft, in apparent terror, then ran from under the scaffold declaring the man was dead, even though he continued to struggle and the vast crowd of onlookers kept yelling and hooting. The Sheriff and other gaol officials were then horror-stricken as Bousfield once again managed to get a foothold on the scaffold.

*The hangman, William Calcraft, acted with unusual haste*

Calcraft was ordered to return. He then went underneath the platform and pulled on the legs for a short time, but on their release the culprit, for a third time, managed to get both his feet astride of the trapdoor. The executioner was compelled to pull the legs below once more, and after a severe struggle Bousfield ceased to exist.

The whole of the awful scene had lasted upwards of ten minutes and the crowd had continually voiced their disapproval. After the body had hung for an hour it was cut down by Calcraft, who was received with groans and hisses.

Later that day it was revealed that Calcraft had received a death threat on the previous Saturday. An anonymous letter had informed him that he would be shot by the Kent Street roughs who wished to put an end to any more executions. This threat had obviously prayed on his mind, and in his haste to clear the scaffold, he had not performed his task with the usual clinical efficiency.

The scaffold scenes had disgusted many of the crowd, and added to the cause for those who wished to rid the nation of such spectacles. It was, however, another twelve years before Calcraft performed the last public execution in May, 1868.

# A Couple of Peculiar Parcels in Whitechapel

On the second Saturday in September, 1875, a man was passing along the Commercial Road, London when he was approached by a young woman who asked him to assist her in carrying some luggage to a cab. He agreed and, on going with her to a house in Queen's Court, was shown two bundles, one of which he placed on his shoulder and carried to the street.

The contents smelt horribly and the man's curiosity being aroused, he turned down the wrappers and discovered that it enclosed a portion of a dead body. The woman carried the other package. When they got to the street they were joined by a man who hailed a passing cab. The man, the woman and the bundles drove rapidly off in the direction of London Bridge.

The man, suspecting foul play, followed the cab and did his best to alert the police. His efforts to keep the cab in sight and at the same time get assistance were unsuccessful until the vehicle had passed over London Bridge into the Borough, where it stopped at an empty house in High Street. At this point he managed to communicate with two police constables who opened the cab door and demanded that the man should inform them of the contents of the parcel. The effluvia arising was unbearable and in order not to attract attention, the officers ordered the cabman to drive to the police-court.

The man, on entering the police-court, suddenly turned pale and the woman trembled in every limb. On the police opening the smaller parcel, which was wrapped in a black piece of American canvas, they were horrified to find the contents consisted of the decomposed trunk of a woman. The man regained his self-possession until the second parcel was opened, when he again became pale. The parcel was larger and the contents were packed in the same manner, but one side was slightly open and from it the fingers of the dead woman were protruding.

The contents of the second bundle consisted of the head of a female, apparently aged mid-twenties, but it was in a very decomposed state and had been covered with lime. The auburn hair had been partially burnt off the crown of the head through the action of the lime, and the eyes were not discernible. Her arms and legs, which had been amputated in a very skilful manner, were also in the parcel.

Following questioning, the man gave his particulars as Henry Wainwright, aged thirty-six, residing at School House Lane, Chingford, Essex, and the woman revealed that she was Alice Day, aged twenty, a dressmaker, living at Queen's Court, Commercial Road. Mr. Wainwright, a manager for a large corn chandler, was charged, along with the young woman, of being in possession of a mutilated body of an adult female, identity unknown.

The goings on of that September evening led to a trial at the Old Bailey that started on the 22nd November, 1875 and lasted for nine days. In the dock were

Henry Wainwright and his brother Thomas, both men being accused of the murder of Harriet Lane, a former governess with a good-class family. As the case unfolded it became apparent that Henry Wainwright was the chief culprit in the affair and that his brother was only a possible accomplice to the matter. It appeared that to all intents and purposes Henry Wainwright had been living a double life.

A good-looking man with handsome features and a beard waved and brushed, he outwardly seemed to have a happy married life with his wife and four children. He had known Harriet Lane for some four years and she had borne him two children while living in rooms provided by him. In her role as mistress he kept her in comparative comfort and enjoyment, giving her as much as £5 per week.

*Henry Wainwright's double life led to a date with the executioner in December, 1875*

However, almost exactly a year before the discovery of the body things had started to go wrong for Henry Wainwright, who found himself in considerable debt. He was living on the edge of a volcano, which threatened to explode at any moment and lead to disastrous consequences, as regards both his domestic and public life.

His mistress was no longer receiving the monetary payments that Henry Wainwright maintained her with and in the middle of September, 1874 she was forced to quit her lodgings in Sidney Square. From then onwards, friends concerned about her well-being were informed by the Wainwright brothers that she had gone away with a man named Edward Friecke. A letter from Brighton, apparently in the handwriting of Thomas Wainwright, and a telegram from Dover saying she was off to Paris followed, in an attempt to pacify the curiosity of those concerned about the woman's disappearance.

Eventually, concern for the woman's safety seemed to diminish and the next significant event was to occur in September 1875. It was then that Henry Wainwright was forced to put up for sale a heavily mortgaged warehouse that he possessed in Whitechapel Road. He knew that in a shallow grave in that building lay the body of Harriet Lane, which he had buried twelve months previously, after he had shot her with his revolver. Fearing that any new tenants may accidentally discover the remains below the floor boards, he determined that the body must have another hiding place. To this end, he cut the corpse up and parcelled it, ready for removal to premises owned by his brother.

The trial showed that Henry Wainwright had purchased chloride in lime with which the body was covered, that he did possess a revolver (the apparent instrument of death) and that the corpse had been concealed at his warehouse premises. It took just less than one hour for the jury to return a verdict. That verdict was that Henry Wainwright was guilty on the charge of wilful murder of Harriet Lane, and that Thomas Wainwright was an accessory after the fact.

The Lord Chief Justice then passed sentence of death upon Henry Wainwright and the prisoner, unmoved, was removed from the dock, casting a far from friendly glance towards his brother.

His Lordship then turned his attention to Thomas Wainwright and informed him that he was sentenced to seven years penal servitude for his part in the unsavoury affair.

The date set for Henry Wainwright's execution was Tuesday the 21st of December, 1875 and during the days that remained his demeanour was one of reckless effrontery. In making a statement about the killing, Wainwright claimed that the crime had been committed by an unnamed man who had been on intimate terms with Harriet Lane and who had fled the country, leaving him to dispose of the remains.

Meanwhile his brother Thomas in his statement claimed that Henry had confessed the murder to him and sought his assistance to dispose of the body.

Whatever the truths that lay in the statement, one woman was determined to save the condemned man from the gallows. She put together a petition which was supported by many signatures and which claimed the verdict was founded on circumstantial evidence. Twenty-four hours before the appointed time, the petition was presented to the Home Secretary. It was not acted upon as the general feeling was that Lord Justice Cockburn had presided over a difficult case in a fair and impartial manner.

As a special favour Henry Wainwright was allowed a cigar the night before his execution. He smoked it in the prison yard, walking up and down with the governor of Newgate Prison. As they walked, they talked and Wainwright recounted his villainies one by one.

His conversation turned to the weaker sex and he calmly assured the governor that no woman could resist him. Throughout his final days he had shown a cool contempt for the consolations of religion and as the hour drew closer he remained impenitent.

That last night he went to bed late, engaged in writing his farewell letters until past one o'clock. He then retired to rest, and slept soundly until ten minutes past four o'clock. An hour later he had breakfast, which consisted simply of a cup of tea. Until the arrival of the Chaplain at six o'clock he spent his time in reading and then his remaining time was spent in devotional exercises.

He submitted to the pinioning operation without a quiver and just three minutes before eight o'clock, being asked if he was ready, he bowed and joined the solemn procession to the death scene.

Ahead of him was William Marwood, the executioner, a trim man with neatly cut whiskers, a decent blue coat and large black tie. His whole face wore an air of business-like complacency.

The spectators and members of the press numbered altogether about two hundred, and when Wainwright appeared on the gallows, pinioned and with a look of helplessness, he excited some sympathy. As he stood thus, his eyes were for a moment lifted and he caught sight of all the eager faces that were watching his last agony. Distinctly his lip curled and a look of contempt passed over his face.

The preparations of the hangman seemed to take an age, yet they lasted only a few seconds. It was as if every moment was an hour as the hangman put the rope around Wainwright's neck. At last the white cap was placed over his head. Marwood retired to a corner, out of sight, and in less than a second the condemned man disappeared out of view into the pit below the drop. The rope swayed for a few moments, very slightly, and in a few minutes more the Governor and others were leaning over the place into which the body had disappeared. All then knew that the life of Henry Wainwright was over.

When his post execution duties were over, executioner William Marwood stated to those still in attendance, that he had never, in all his experience, met a criminal who faced death with such fortitude and calmness.

### Postscript
After the execution Alice Day who, after initial enquiries, had been cleared of any connection with the crime, announced that the story of her life was now ready, written by herself. It was a pamphlet of 16 pages entitled *From the footlights to the Prison Cell* and it cost one penny. The pamphlet recorded her strange eventual history as "Promptress, fairy in a pantomime, pet of the ballet, circus rider, sculptor's model and, lately, charged in the dock with the Whitechapel Murderer".

# Little Ada Murdered in Acton Town

In the autumn of 1880 there lived in Cowper Place, Acton, in a house called 'Herbert Villa', a family by the name of Shepheard. The family was a happy one and consisted of John Shepheard, who was a house decorator, his wife and their five children, the eldest being a girl called Ada who was eleven years of age.

Mr. Shepheard was successful in his trade, and to aid him in his labours he employed a man called George Pavey, who was a painter. The house decorator trusted his employee, who was partially disabled, and occasionally he would carry out work in the Shepheard family home.

One such occasion was Friday the 22nd of October, 1880, on which day Mr. and Mrs. Shepheard left home shortly before noon in order to transact some business in the city. Before they left they asked George Pavey if he would take care of Ada, who was at home, and the other children when they returned from school at lunch time. A couple of hours after the parents had departed, Ada and her sisters were seen in the neighbourhood, buying sweets and nuts, before the younger children returned to school.

Mr. Shepheard and his wife were delayed on their business and returned home at six thirty that evening. When they approached the house they were surprised to find the place in darkness. Entering by the front door, they proceeded to the kitchen, all the while calling for Pavey and the children. The kitchen door was locked, but the key was on the outside.

Unlocking the door, the couple entered the room and to their horror saw their daughter Ada lying dead upon the hearth rug. The body was lying perfectly straight, with the legs towards the door and with an handkerchief over the girl's face. Her throat had been cut. By her side was a bag of nuts.

The parents immediately raised the alarm and to their relief their other children were found safe in a neighbour's house. The doctor who was sent for observed the stab wound in the neck which had led to death. He also discovered that the child had been violated.

A police constable who hurried to the house saw a table knife on the dresser and, being covered in blood, it was adjudged to be the murder weapon. On going upstairs the constable noticed that a back bedroom door had been forced open. In that room was a cash box which had been opened with a screwdriver. When shown the cash box by the constable, Mr. Shepheard explained that it had, until that morning when he had taken the money with him, held £150 for a house sale. It was his belief that Pavey had thought the money was still in the cash box, having discussed it with him the previous day.

Police and public alike at once went in search of George Pavey, who had been seen shortly after three o'clock that afternoon in his shirt sleeves on the Birkbeck Road, heading in the direction of the Uxbridge Road. A police inspector was dispatched to Pavey's lodgings in Notting Hill, where his wife and child resided, but the man did not return that night. He was eventually discovered on the Sunday evening at Hendon Workhouse and taken to Paddington police station.

On the following morning he was taken to the police court to be examined and when shown the handkerchief discovered at the scene, he replied that it was his and he had put it there. He then went on to make a statement to the effect that, while he was at the house, a man had called and told him that his master was at the Uxbridge Road railway station and wished to see him urgently. Believing the story, he hurried to the station and when he returned found the child lying murdered and violated. He placed his handkerchief over her face and left the house through fear that he should be accused of the crime, knowing that he had been convicted of an indecent assault before.

*Executioner William Marwood*

Exactly a month after his arrest George Pavey, aged 29, appeared in the Central Criminal Court before Mr. Justice Hawkins, accused of the wilful murder of Ada Shepheard. He pleaded, 'Not Guilty', in a firm manner and his defence was based on the claim that a mysterious stranger had been responsible.

Amongst the witnesses called was the distraught father of the dead child and he related the tragic events to the attentive members of the jury. A surgeon of the Metropolitan Police Force told the court that he had examined the prisoner's clothing and found bloodstains upon his shirt collar and his waistcoat. The defence Counsel, in response, suggested that the blood had come from the prisoner having a nose bleed.

The prosecution, at the conclusion of its evidence, claimed that the crime had been brought home to the prisoner clearly and conclusively. The Defence Counsel argued that the evidence was purely circumstantial and that Pavey's claim that another person was responsible was a highly feasible one. He then cited a notorious murder case at Denham, where a family of seven had been killed by a man who had tricked his way into the premises in a similar way to that claimed by his client.

The jury were clearly unimpressed by the Defence Counsel's arguments for they took only a few minutes to return with a 'Guilty' verdict. Mr. Justice Hawkins then asked the prisoner if he had anything to say before sentence was passed and he chose to make no reply. His Lordship then placed the black cap upon his head and addressed George Pavey in a solemn manner, saying:

"It is impossible to conceive a more atrocious or cruel crime than that of which you have been convicted. God knows what could have possessed you to commit that atrocious cruelty in violating the poor helpless girl and afterwards to murder her in the most cruel and brutal manner.

You must, young as you are, prepare to die, for your crime is of so barbarous a nature that I do not hold out any hope of a reprieve".

His Lordship, who was much affected, then passed sentence of death in the usual manner. The prisoner heard the sentence with perfect composure and walked from the dock with a firm step.

The execution of Pavey was arranged for the second Monday in December, 1880, and during his final days he confessed his crime and admitted the justice of his sentence. Three days before his death he was visited by his wife and child and expressed his regret for the situation he had left them in.

Executioner William Marwood was summoned to Newgate gaol to carry out the execution. Pavey showed great firmness upon the scaffold and death was almost instantaneous. Later that day an inquest was held and that night the convict was buried within the precincts of the gaol.

# To Disappear in London's Crowded Streets

One of the most notorious criminals of the nineteenth century was Charles Frederick Peace. Born in Sheffield in 1832 he was partly crippled as a boy following an accident which left him with a limp. By the time he was twenty, he had developed into an agile and enormously strong individual who had embarked on a career of burglary and theft. He made the perfect cat-burglar, capable of moving silently and swiftly across the roof tops to plunder the upper rooms of wealthy establishments.

A versatile and elusive character, he went from town to town using an old violin case to carry the tools of his trade. His crimes, however, were not always undetected and on at least four occasions he was apprehended and subjected to terms of imprisonment.

In 1872, by which time he was married to a widow who had a son, he returned to his Sheffield roots and set up in business as a dealer in old musical instruments and as a picture framer and gilder. Despite his apparent respectability, his appearance and his talent with the violin, he remained a compulsive cat-burglar.

Eventually, in 1876 things began to go terribly wrong for him. Firstly, while about to rob a fashionable house in Manchester, he was surprised by a police officer. Desperate to avoid capture, he fired at Police Constable Nicholas Cock and struck him a fatal blow in the chest.

During the same period Peace was forcing his unwelcome attention on Katherine Dyson, the young wife of a Sheffield neighbour. The summer of 1876 brought the situation to a head after Peace had threatened the life of Katherine Dyson and her husband Arthur. Subsequently a Magistrates Warrant was issued for his arrest and Peace uprooted his family and headed for Hull, the matter being dropped.

However, as summer turned to autumn Peace turned up on the doorstep of the Dyson's new home in another neighbourhood of Sheffield. Mrs. Dyson wished to have nothing to do with the small, slight man, who looked older than his years, with grey hair and a distinctive speech impediment. Arthur Dyson attempted to make it clear to Peace that his wife did not desire his attention.

Such was Peace's obsession, however, that a month or so later, while in an intoxicated state, he once more knocked on the door of the Dyson's home. That evening, almost inevitably, a violent scene ensued and Arthur Dyson attempted to chase Peace away from the neighbourhood. As they went down a passageway two shots were fired, Dyson being hit in the head and dying almost instantly.

Peace fled from the scene of his latest crime and within days a reward had been posted for his apprehension on the capital charge. His hope was to disappear amongst the crowded streets of London and to this end he set himself up in

Peckham, as a gentleman of independent means. He appeared both respectable and hospitable and when a series of burglaries began to occur in the vicinity, none suspected the violin playing Mr. Thompson who attended church regularly with his wife.

All went well until one night in October, 1878 when a constable on duty in Blackheath noticed a flickering light in a prosperous house. The constable called for assistance and when Peace emerged from the drawing room window he was confronted by the police officers. The chase was on, five shots rang out from Peace's pistol and one officer was hit in the arm. Peace was finally overpowered and arrested. The police were unaware that they had caught the wanted man, Peace, and under his assumed name of John Ward he was tried at the Old Bailey. Despite his pleas for mercy he received the full force of the law and was sentenced to penal servitude for life.

As he began his sentence the police began to unravel the mystery of the Blackheath burglar, and information from family or foe led to the realisation that he was not only the affable Mr. Thompson, but also the notorious Charles Peace. As a consequence he was at once charged with the murder of Arthur Dyson and plans were made to transfer him to Sheffield for a hearing before the Magistrates.

In the company of two warders from Pentonville he was taken on a London express bound for Sheffield. Throughout the journey the manacled Peace was in an agitated state and made numerous requests to visit the water closet. At Peterborough the warders were induced to allow him to leave the carriage, but he became so violent at that station that it was with some difficulty that they got him back on board the train.

The situation then eased until the train was between Shireoaks Station and Kiveton Park, a locality with which the prisoner was perfectly familiar, being only some fifteen miles from Sheffield. At this point the window was opened for his convenience and seizing the opportunity, Peace leapt up at the open window and threw himself bodily through the gap. The officer nearest the window made a lunge for him and was able to catch him by the leg, the head of the convict being down on the outside of the foot board.

A fearful struggle commenced with Peace endeavouring to shake off the warder with his other leg, and at the same time use his hands, although manacled, as a lever against the foot board in an endeavour to force the warder to release his hold. The other officer was unable, owing to the narrowness of the window, to render much assistance, but tried to communicate with the driver and the guard. This he was unable to do, owing to the communication cord not being in good working order. The struggle outside the carriage was seen, however, by some of the passengers, and the driver's attention was obtained after the struggle had continued for some two miles.

The officer bravely held on although considerably exhausted, and it was not until the boot of the convict gave way that the warder was compelled to relax his hold.

Peace then fell down on to his head and shortly afterwards the train was brought to a halt. There was no time for discussion between the warders or the train's officials and it was impossible for the train to go back because, with another engine due in twenty minutes, there would have been grave danger of a collision. Therefore, the train was ordered to continue on it's journey and the warders and a few of the passengers hurried back down the line to see if anything could be seen of Peace.

After proceeding for about a mile they found him lying insensible, close to the rails, and bleeding profusely from the head. The next train, a slow one from Worksop, was signalled and Peace was placed in the guard's van. He lay almost unconscious, muttering only the occasional sentence.

When the train arrived at Sheffield he had to be carried into the prison van by four men and after being taken to the Town Hall, he was removed to the cells. He was in an very exhausted state, but after a little while he spoke a few words to the warders, and took a pretty stiff dose of brandy, which was administered to him on medical orders. He was found to be suffering from a severely lacerated scalp wound, and from shock and concussion of the brain.

When he had made his leap from the train it was travelling at the rate of 40 miles an hour, and if the officer had not caught him, it was felt that it would have been a fatal action on behalf of Peace. The following morning a piece of paper was found in the coat of the convict and upon it was written, "Bury me at Darnell. God Bless you all. C. Peace". This discovery led the authorities to believe that the object of his leap was not escape, but suicide.

By a singular occurrence he had made the leap very near to the place he asked to be buried. Another minute or two and the train would have torn past the old church at Darnell, near to which Peace had formerly lived. There he had occupied a detached house which stood in its own grounds. It was in the village that he had formed the acquaintance of the Dysons, persecuted Mrs. Dyson with his attention, and finally threatened to shoot her. He always, in fact, spoke of Darnell as his home and frequently expressed a desire to be buried there.

*Charles Frederick Peace – no hiding place in London*

Within days Peace had made a rapid recovery from his injuries, and it was hoped that he would be fit enough to stand trial at the next Leeds Assizes following his committal by the Sheffield Magistrates.

The key witness at the trial was Mrs. Dyson who, after her husband's death, had been living in America. Determined to see the ends of justice complete, she had travelled back to England in time to identify Peace at the Sheffield hearings.

Prior to the Assizes, Peace was held in Armley gaol and at the trial at the end of January, 1879, he partially walked and was partially carried up the steps into the dock, before being placed in a chair with warders either side of him. He appeared most pitiable, being so weak he could barely sit up in his chair. On the charge being read to him, he pleaded 'Not Guilty', but he spoke in so low a tone he could hardly be heard.

Much depended on the testimony of Mrs. Dyson who told the court how Peace had pursued her, even when they had moved to Banner Cross. She then related how Peace had cold-bloodedly shot her husband.

In his defence the representatives of Peace claimed that a struggle had taken place between the two men and that the pistol had gone off accidentally. Peace, it was claimed, had no intention of killing Dyson, a man who had developed an intense jealousy due to the accused man's affection for his wife.

The jury were unimpressed by the pleas on behalf of Peace and took only ten minutes to find him 'Guilty as charged'. At that point His Lordship informed Charles Peace that the punishment was the sentence of death.

While awaiting execution, Peace made a full confession of his crimes and this included the shooting of P.C. Cock, the Manchester policeman. As a result his confession of the murder was transmitted to the Home Secretary. This led to the eventual pardon of William Habron, who was serving a life sentence for that crime.

In one of the letters he wrote as he awaited execution, he stated that, "God and myself alone know all the dreadful crimes I have done".

The execution was set for Tuesday, the 25th February, 1879, at Armley Gaol, Leeds. That morning he woke at a quarter to six o'clock. At a quarter to seven breakfast was taken to his cell and an hour later the prison bell began to toll. Four representatives of the press were placed within view of the scaffold and they saw the solemn procession led by the governor of the gaol. The culprit was led by two warders and behind him was William Marwood, the executioner.

Peace walked firmly and cast his eyes to the gallows, but before Marwood could continue his work, Peace addressed the press reporters. Without the slightest sign of nervousness, he informed them that his life had been 'base and bad' but that he felt assured that his sins had been forgiven him and that the Kingdom of Heaven awaited.

He then turned towards Marwood and said, "I am ready if you are". The executioner then pulled the white cap over his face, adjusted the rope and sprang to the lever. As the bolt was drawn, the drop fell and Peace died without a struggle.

A memorial card was produced which quoted Charles Peace as saying, "I was executed. Aged 47. For that I done but never intended".

# A Desperate Intruder at Highfield House

The burglar who goes armed to his work is regarded in a different light than the sneak thief who, once in a while, breaks a pane of glass or forces back the weak bolt of a door in order to gain his plunder.

In the year 1882 the public awareness of the burglar was high, following an increase in the number of household robberies reported by the Metropolitan Police Commissioner. Therefore, great public interest was shown in the events of a night early in September, 1882.

On that evening Clara Emily Reynolds, the mistress of Highfield House, Stamford Hill, Hackney, was disturbed in her relaxation by noises from the first floor. She was not alone and at once went into the billiard room where two guests were engaged in a game. The visitors, at her request, searched about the front and back of the premises and found a ladder leaning against one of the first floor windows.

The first thing they did was to take away the ladder to thwart the intruder's means of escape. Meanwhile Mrs. Reynolds and the groom, Robert Howe, made their way cautiously up the stairs, but before they had reached the landing a man appeared at a bedroom door and fired a revolver in their direction. They at once stopped in their tracks and the burglar brushed past them. His escape route, however, was not a clear one because the two guests, Thomas Munday and Edward Haselden, had returned indoors and begun to climb the staircase. The man immediately pointed his revolver at Mr. Munday and fired two shots, both of which, fortunately, missed their target.

Mr. Haselden who had an unloaded fowling piece in his possession, raised it upwards and struck the intruder with the butt end. The burglar responded by once more firing his revolver and two bullets whistled through Mr. Haselden's coat tails.

At this point the groom was stirred into action and, grabbing hold of the intruder, he tussled with him until the balustrade gave way and the pair of them fell off the stairway onto the floor. When they landed the groom was uppermost and the intruder responded by firing a shot upwards at Robert Howe, the bullet entering the breast. The shot was less than an inch from his heart and passed clean through his body, lodging itself in the ceiling. At this point the burglar was overpowered and the weapon taken from his grasp.

The police were called immediately and the man was identified as labourer, John Saunders. In his possession were found four rings, a gold watch and other articles valued at more than £50. He seemed to show no regret for his actions, remarking that he had meant to kill Mr. Haselden for hitting him with the butt of his gun, and stating that, had the revolver worked properly, he would have killed the lot of them. To highlight his callous indifference, he looked towards Howe, who lay drenched in blood, and said, "I have given him what he will never get over".

Fortunately for Howe, owing to his strong constitution and the skill of the surgeon, he made a remarkable recovery after his life had been in peril for some time. In consequence Saunders was regarded as lucky to not be facing a capital charge when he stood in the dock of the Central Criminal Court in mid October, 1882.

Amongst the charges he faced before Mr. Justice Watkin Williams was one of intent to murder Robert Howe and of shooting at the others present on that September night. At the outset of the proceedings he pleaded guilty to the charge of burglary at Highfield House and to a similar robbery at another fashionable London home.

Attention was then drawn to the shooting incidents and the actions of the cornered criminal, in his attempt to flee, were brought before the jury. It was also stated that a search had been made of Saunder's lodgings and there 150 ball cartridges and another revolver had been found. The prosecution reminded the court that the prisoner had gone to commit burglary armed with a loaded revolver, a weapon to endanger the life of anyone who may try to arrest him, be it a householder or a policeman.

In his defence, Saunders stated that he had never intended to use the revolver to kill, but only to frighten anyone who might stop him. He also denied using the expressions that it was claimed he uttered with regard to those who captured him and, finally, he said the pistol had gone off accidentally in the struggle with Howe.

The jury took little time to find John Saunders 'Guilty' of shooting with intent to murder and His Lordship then began the process of sentencing.

He addressed the prisoner in a solemn manner and told Saunders that he was unable to distinguish his crime from that of Wilful Murder. He continued that it was perfectly intolerable in a great city like London that people such as Saunders should be at large. In conclusion he said that, in his humble judgement, society had a right to demand that "they should be rid of your presence for the rest of your life". The 29 year old Saunders was then informed he would be kept in penal servitude for life.

# A Fatal Passion for Sightseeing

Half an hour before noon on the third Tuesday of June, 1898, the Duchess of York, who was accompanied by the Duke, the future King George V, and other dignitaries left the Speaker's Steps at Westminster on board the *Beatrice*, a vessel belonging to the London County Council. The Duchess was on her way to launch the battleship *Albion* at the Thames Ironworks at Blackwell.

The ships lying in the river between Tower Bridge and Blackwell were, for the most part, gaily decked with bunting, and almost immediately after the Royal party started their journey the sun came out and added to the gaiety of the scene.

The entrance to the shipbuilding yard was also decorated profusely with bunting and the *Albion* was covered with flags. The Royal party were greeted with cheers as the *Beatrice* steamed in to the creek. Their Royal Highnesses' were received by the Chairman of the shipbuilding company, who presided at a lunch attended by some three hundred guests.

In proposing a toast, "Success to the *Albion* and the health of the Duchess of York", the Chairman offered his hearty thanks to her for her attendance. The Duke, affectionately known as the 'Sailor Prince', in reply, referred to the fact that the first Ironclad for the British Navy had been constructed at the Thames Ironworks in 1859, adding that since that date many famous ships had been launched from the yard. He congratulated the company on their achievements and expressed the hope that the *Albion* would prove as successful as previous ships.

The Royal party then proceeded to the head-staging, where it was apparent that the launch was about to be witnessed by many thousands of people. Stands had been erected around the slipway, and the stagings around the other ships under construction in the yard were all crowded with sightseers, as were the roofs of the surrounding buildings.

After the usual service had been conducted by Bishop Barry, the last stays were knocked away from beneath the ship and, on a signal being given, the Duchess was handed a knife and asked to sever the cord holding the ship. At the second attempt the Duchess succeeded in cutting the rope and the ship slowly moved away. Her Royal Highness then duly christened the vessel.

A loud cheer greeted the first perceptible motion of the vessel and as the fine ship slowly slid down the spillway, increasing her velocity every moment, the crowd waved their hats and cheered. The steam vessels in the creek greeted their new comrade with shrill blasts on their steam whistles. The launch was executed magnificently, notwithstanding the difficulties of the very small amount of room in the creek, and the vessel was slowly brought up by four immensely thick warps.

The Thames Ironworks Company had two construction yards on a crescent shaped inlet of the Thames called Bow Creek. The yard furthest from the river, was used for the construction of the *Albion*. The other yard, about a couple of hundred yards or so nearer the river, had been assigned to the building of the still larger Japanese battleship *Shiki-Shima*, which was expected to be launched in the October.

The exit from the yard containing the Japanese war vessel had been closed up by a kind of wooden well, built to last for two years, the period of the ship's construction. The well also served the purpose of a gangway between the two wharves. Boards had been put up to warn spectators of the danger of crowding on to this wooden structure, and several policemen had been stationed at either end of the gangway to keep it clear, or at least prevent it from being overcrowded.

Alas, a crowd on such occasions thinks less of its safety than of gratifying, at all risks, its passion for sightseeing, and the consequence was that the multitude on the wharves pushed their impetuous way past policemen and danger posts and took possession of the gangway in large numbers. It was the best of all places for seeing the mammoth battleship plunge down from the slips and along the crescent-shaped creek to the river, and to this coign of vantage the crowd pushed its way.

It was a fine moment when, amid the blare of music, the cheers of the spectators, and the deafening uproar of jubilant sirens and steam whistles, the ironclad monster glided down and took a header into the water, which was at its highest tidal mark. Not yet fully equipped, the *Albion* was reckoned to have a displacement of 7,000 tons and this enormous weight in the creek caused a violent shoreward movement of the water, which rose and dashed with most destructive force against the wooden gangway structure, shaking and shattering it as if it had been a mere matchbox.

A scene of terrible confusion ensued, the shrieks of the drowning mingling with the cheers of the thousands who were quite unaware of the accident. The police boats instantly made for the spot, and with the aid of many dockyard hands several people were pulled out of the water, whilst many scrambled out themselves.

The unfortunate people who were thrown into the water were for the most part inhabitants of the neighbourhood, the wives and daughters of dockyard hands. Several persons who were taken out in an apparently lifeless condition were conveyed to the sheds in the yards and attended to there. Several bodies were then hauled out quite dead, one of the first being a baby.

Firemen and several nurses were soon on the scene and hot coffee and brandy were freely administered to the half drowned girls and women. Amongst those most active in the rescue work were members of the Thames Police Force who organised the willing volunteers and worked with vigour and intelligence.

Meanwhile, heart rendering scenes were taking place at the approaches to the yard as the wildest rumours soon got abroad. Everyone who had friends in the yard rushed to obtain news of them – mothers sought their sons and daughters, husbands their wives and brothers their sisters. Some ran about wildly, asking everybody they met for news of their friends, and many touching scenes occurred when some lost one was found to be safe.

By seven o'clock that night the bodies of thirty victims had been recovered and brought ashore from the muddy water below the wrecked stage. At an improvised mortuary the bodies were placed in long straight rows, and then husbands, wives and fathers passed slowly along, endeavouring to identify their missing relatives.

So sudden was the disaster that the chief guests on the stands at the head of the ship were totally unaware that any accident had occurred, and the majority had left Blackwell on the return journey without having heard of the news. This was the case with the Duke and Duchess of York, who did not receive any tidings of the calamity until after their return to York House. The Duke then immediately telegraphed the Chairman of the Thames Ironwork Company, expressing his deep regret at the terrible disaster, and his sympathy with the relatives and friends of those who had lost their lives.

At the subsequent inquests the police reported that the crowds increased to such an extent that they were overpowered, their warnings were disregarded and the officers were powerless to clear them from the bridge.

The final coroner's inquiry into 33 victims of the disaster recorded a verdict of 'Accidental Death'. No blame was attached to anyone, but it was recommended that on future occasions greater precautions should be taken to keep the public in bounds. The jury exonerated the police from any laxity in carrying out their instructions and praised the brave fellows who risked their lives to save others.

# Mary Baked a Poisoned Cake

Towards the end of September, 1898, a domestic servant called Mary Ann Ansell insured her sister's life for the sum of £22, at a cost of three pence per week. Her sister Caroline was, in fact, an inmate of the Leavesden Asylum in Watford and Mary, who was 21 years old, told her mother that she had insured her sister's life to ensure that if anything happened to her, she would be able to give her a nice funeral.

On the 9th of March in the following year Caroline received a parcel, by post, which contained a cake. After eating it, Caroline, who was four years older than her sister, became very ill and five days later she died from phosphorous poisoning.

Within a couple of days Mary wrote to the insurance agent informing him of her sister's untimely death. The insurance money was refused and inquiries were at once made into the circumstances of the death. The outcome was that, early in April, Mary was arrested and accused of killing her sister.

At the subsequent trial of Mary Ann Ansell it was shown that she had bought phosphorous poison, and a long serious of coincidences connected her with the crime, including the posting of the cake and the forging of a letter from her mother protesting at the carrying out of a post mortem on Caroline. Called into the witness box Mary coolly denied all knowledge of the poisoned cake, but she was found guilty.

*Mr Juctice Matthews*
*(from an 1892 'Leisure Hour')*

His Lordship, Mr. Justice Matthews told her, "It is impossible for a jury of reasonable and conscientious men to return any other verdict. You were moved to this terrible crime for the sake of the small sum of money which you would receive on the policy of insurance. Never, in my experience, has so terrible a crime been committed for a motive so totally inadequate". He concluded by sentencing her to be hanged and telling her to prepare to follow her victim to an early grave.

Certain newspapers in London at once threw themselves into an agitation for the reprieve of the condemned woman. Their columns teemed with appeals for mercy from all kinds of people, including some members of the jury who had found her guilty. The excuse made by the agitators was that Mary Ann Ansell was insane, and the Home Secretary duly arranged for a couple of eminent doctors to examine her. Upon their finding he declined to advise the Crown to interfere with the due course of the law.

Despite his decision, the agitators for a reprieve went to extraordinary lengths to save the condemned woman's life and a deputation went to Windsor Castle in the hope of gaining Queen Victoria's sympathy. Her Majesty, who had received numerous pleas by letter, refused to grant them an audience and referred them to the Home Secretary.

With time running out the petitioners obtained the support of over a hundred Members of Parliament, but this late attempt to sway the Home Secretary was unsuccessful. On hearing of the Home Secretary's decision, one member of the jury remarked, "I am deeply upset at seeing the decision of the Home Secretary to hang Mary Ansell. Although we were bringing in a verdict of guilty, we had no idea she would really be hanged".

The execution of Mary Ann Ansell took place on a sunny morning in mid July, 1899 at St. Alban's Gaol, and the hangman was James Billington. The condemned woman seemed scarcely to realise up to the last that she would be executed, holding tenaciously to the belief that a reprieve would be granted. Only when the procession to the scaffold was formed did her last hope vanish and, in a distressed state, the bolt fell and she was launched into eternity.

A large well behaved crowd had gathered outside the prison and as the black flag was hoisted, shortly after eight o'clock that morning, many of Mary's petitioners knelt in prayer. Later that day one prison official was interviewed by the press and he remarked, "I do not think she was insane. In all my dealings with her I have come to the conclusion that her demeanour was more sullen than anything else".

# All At Sea, on board
# The 'Flowery Land'

On the 28th of July, 1863, a vessel named *Flowery Land* left London bound for Singapore, with a cargo of wine and other goods. Her captain was John Smith, an Englishman, and there were four other Englishmen on board, including the first mate, Karswell and the second mate, Taffir. The rest of the crew were a polyglot lot and most of them turned out to be blackguards of the deepest dye. Half a dozen were Spaniards, or rather natives of Manila, and men of colour; one was Greek, another of Turkish origin; there was also a Frenchman; a carpenter from Norway; three of Chinese nationality and others of dubious origins.

In all it was a nondescript crew and in consequence navigation and discipline was far from easy. The captain was a kindly soul, but a man of intemperate habits. The first mate, a man of dogged determination, was the one who shouldered the responsibility of seeing the daily duties carried out. To ensure that the crew stuck to their tasks, he freely handed out punishments such as 'rope's ending' and 'tying to the bulwarks'.

Now it so happened that the Greek, the Turk and the six Spaniards were assigned to the same watch and, as the days at sea turned into weeks, they began to brood over the punishments being handed out to all and sundry. They were eight truculent and reckless scoundrels who, burning for revenge, hatched amongst themselves a plot to kill the officers and seize the vessel.

The mutiny was planned in the utmost secrecy and began in the middle of the night on the 10th of September. At the same time an attack was made upon the Captain and the first mate. One half of the mutineers approached the first mate, Karswell, who was on watch on the deck, whilst the others headed for the captain's quarters to rouse him from his slumbers. Armed with handspikes and capstan-bars the mutineers made their murderous attack on the first mate. Despite his pleas for mercy they beat him about the head and face until every feature was obliterated, and then, as he still breathed, they flung him into the sea.

No sooner had the Captain emerged from his cabin, clad in his night-shirt, than a cluster of mutineers surrounded him and promptly despatched him from this life with a series of dagger wounds, which they inflicted with cold and cruel ferocity.

Their attention was next reserved for the Captain's brother who was a passenger on the vessel. He also felt the full fury of the night time assassins, who stabbed him to death with the same daggers that had ended the Captain's life, and, like his brother, he was thrown into the deep.

The second mate, Taffir, had heard the agonising cries and, catching sight of the mutineers, he fled into his quarters in fear of his life. His berth was soon surrounded by the frightening mob who, conscious of his usefulness, informed him they would spare his life if he would navigate the ship to the River Plate or Buenos Ayres.

Immediately after the mutiny was complete, the mutineers ransacked the Captain's cabin and divided the money and clothes amongst themselves. They then raided the cargo hold and cases of champagne were brought on deck and broached to celebrate their bloody coup. The Spaniard, Leon, wished to make everyone on board share the spoils, so as to implicate the innocent with the guilty but Varto, the Turk, would not allow any but the eight mutineers to have anything.

For nearly three weeks the ship continued her voyage with the mutineers in control, and on the second day of October land was sighted some ten miles distant. When nightfall arrived they determined to scuttle the vessel and disembark on the ship's boats.

All the crew were permitted to leave except for the three Chinese who had been roughly treated since the mutiny. One of them was thrown into the water and drowned and the other two were left to go down with the ship. They were last seen clinging to the tops as the waters closed over them.

The boats reached the shore on the 4th of October, at a place not far from the entrance to the River Plate. Leon had prepared a plausible tale to the effect that they had belonged to an American ship from Peru, bound for Bordeaux, which had floundered at sea; that they had been in the boats five days and nights, and that the Captain and others had been lost.

A farmer took them in for the night and drove them next day to Rocha, a place north of Maldonado. At that point Taffir took the opportunity to make his escape from the mutineers' clutches and, after a twenty mile journey, gave information of the mutiny to the Brazilian authorities.

As a consequence the mutineers were arrested, the case inquired into by a naval court martial, and the prisoners eventually handed over to the British authorities, who arranged their passage back to England and to confinement in Newgate gaol.

Their trial followed at the Central Criminal Court, all eight being arraigned at the same time. In the dock were six Spaniards, Leon, Blanco, Lopez, Duranno, Santos and, Marsolino; the Turk called Vartos and the Greek named Carlos.

Carlos was acquitted and the other seven all found guilty of murder on the high seas. Of those Santos and Marsolino were reprieved and their sentences commuted to penal servitude for life, the other five were sentenced to death.

The date reserved for their execution was Monday the 22nd of February, 1864. It was to take place, outside Newgate gaol. The crime committed by the pirates of the *Flowery Land* had been cold-blooded in its conception and brutal in it's execution and, as a result, there was not a tinge of sympathy for the murderers.

During the whole of the Sunday, the space in front of Newgate gaol was flocked to by throngs of men, women and children. As evening closed in, the crowd grew denser, and at the same time changed its character. Detachments of roughs of the lowest order began to arrive, and while the greater number wandered listlessly about, some of the more patient and determined spirits took up their positions, intent on holding them until all was over. There were many women in the throng, some young in years but old in vice, and children of the lowest class were in abundance. They clambered upon the barriers and exchanged callous remarks about the coming show which sounded hideous in the tiny tones of infancy.

There were some redeeming features in the scene for a few good men endeavoured to turn the occasion to pious account. City preachers, itinerant preachers, and temperance orators sought to pour warning and counsel upon hardened ears; but riotous gaiety was the prevailing characteristic of the scene. The whole of the neighbourhood of the prison wore the aspect of a fair, the pie men and vendors of baked potatoes seeming to be doing a roaring trade.

As the night wore on the brutal element in the mob showed itself more and more prominently. Yells and execrations poured forth, expressing innate ferocity. Many of those with tickets for windows were seriously maltreated and plundered of everything he had been foolish enough to carry in their pockets. One victim even had the hat removed from his head, while an attempt was made to steal the trousers of another.

Fresh numbers continued to pour into the gaols vicinity from the slums of Southwark, the dens of St. Giles's, the sinks of Somerstown, and the purliens of Whitechapel. Costermongers rubbed shoulders with dapper clerks and shop-boys, and screaming women blasphemed at the tipsy men. Roughs reviled each other at safe distance and bedraggled women in gaudy rags pushed about with more than masculine effrontery. With continued additions to the crowd, with increasing blasphemy from the roughs, the Sunday faded away, and there came the black Monday of 1864.

Hitherto the occupants of the rooms facing Newgate gaol had kept their blinds down, but no sooner had the chime of midnight died on the ear, than the blinds were pulled up and the windows in most of the houses opened. Those who had been able to pay for 'reserved seats' sought amusement in watching those standing on the cold ground. Having paid the extravagant price demanded, they settled themselves coolly to wait for the death struggles of five fellow creatures. Many were coarse people with plenty of money and very little feeling. Yet many were the so called exemplars of society and as they waited they feasted on fowls, hams, tongue and sandwiches; washed down with potent liquors, especially champagne and sherry. They whiled away the hours playing cards and smoking the best cigars money could buy.

Conspicuous amongst the lovers of cruel pleasures were a knot of officers of the Guards who, in the absence of any opportunity of looking upon battlefield slaughter, seized upon the chance of observing another form of homicide.

A few minutes before three o'clock a team of powerful horses appeared, dragging behind them the base of the scaffold. Hooting, cat-calls and yells greeted the men employed in erecting the mechanism of death. A busy hour was spent and by four o'clock the huge structure, surmounted by the beam to which were attached five dangling chains, stretched from the debtors' door of Newgate prison.

One change had been introduced: the drop was surrounded up to a height of two feet with black drape cloth, above which only the heads of the culprits would be seen after the bolt was drawn. The mob were evidently quite unprepared for this innovation in metropolitan hangings and resented it bitterly. The moment the workmen began to place the cloth a storm of yells and hisses arose and it did not subdue until the stoutest-lungs had exhausted their breath.

By six o'clock the crowd had increased still further, and on this hazy morning it was estimated that not less than thirty thousand had arrived to fix their gaze upon the gallows. Before another hour passed executioner William Calcraft appeared on the scaffold and in his hands he carried the halters for the five condemned convicts. As he threw them down upon the platform he was greeted with many hisses, mingled with cheers, and responded to both with a look of contemptuous indifference.

As eight o'clock drew ever nearer, the one noticeable characteristic of the mob was its hilarity and light-hearted spirit. There was scarcely anyone in the crowd who wasn't in a holiday spirit and few gave thought for the doomed wretches who

*A Newgate execution scene similar to this earlier one was desired by the gathered multitude – but on the day in February, 1864, a black drape cloth partially hid the victims from view*

were separated from eternity by only a few minutes. The dull roar of the huge multitude was a sound never to be forgotten and it's tone was of unmixed jollity and rough enjoyment.

At one minute past eight Calcraft appeared on the scaffold followed by the convict Blanco. By an error of judgement, altogether inconceivable, the hangman placed the first culprit under that portion of the beam which was nearest the prison. He then followed the same rule in dealing with the remainder, so that each man had to pass by his companions with the cap drawn over their faces and the rope around their necks.

Blanco stood firmly until the noose had been adjusted and hooked on to the chain, but as the cap was drawn down his courage failed him. He fell into a state

## Murder on Board The 'Flowery Land'

Oh! what numbers did flock to see
Five murderers die on the gallows tree,
For those cruel deeds which they have done,
Their fatal glass is now quite run;
When they were sent to the shades below,
No tears of pity for them did flow,
No mercy did they expect to have,
Only to fill a murderer's grave.
Those five men on the drop did stand
For their deeds on board the 'Flowery Land'.

Children and mothers they have caused to weep,
For those who were slain and sunk in the deep;
We hope they are number'd with the blest,
And with God above their souls at rest;
Their sufferings were great, no tongue can tell,
Welt'ring in blood, on the deck they fell.
On their knees, for mercy they did crave.
But were murder'd and sunk beneath the waves.

They've took from wives their husbands dear.
And griev'd their hearts the sad news to hear.
But in the hour of their distress,
God protect them and the fatherless!
For what those murderers did on board the
   'Flowery Land'
At the throne of God they will have to stand.
On the scaffold their lives did forfeit pay,
Oh, what will they feel on the Judgement day.

In the mighty deep, where the billows roar
Their victims sleep for evermore,
Tho' they patted them from those they love
We hope their friends will meet them in Heaven
   above,
Where their sufferings will be all o'er
On another bless'd and peaceful shore,
Where they will feel no grief or pain,
But for every dwell ne'er to part again.

In the murderers' last hour, the solemn bell,
Warn'd them to bid this world farewell,
To resign their breath they did on the gallows
   stand,
Life for life's required by God and man;
The murderers on the fatal morn,
On the gallows did die, expos'd to scorn,
For there was no sympathy,
When they were launched in eternity.

We hope that this will a warning be,
To all, either by land or sea,
From the paths of virtue never to stray,
And never take precious life away;
Or like those mutineers, your fate may be,
Have to end your days on the fatal tree,
No one for them could pity have,
When they were sent to the murderer's grave.

of entire collapse and swayed about, half kneeling and hanging with his full weight upon the halter. The exhortations of the Catholic chaplain and the Under Sheriffs were all in vain and at last a chair was brought upon the platform, upon which the wretched man sat, a huddled up and trembling heap of half-dead humanity.

One by one his comrades passed by him prepared for death. Firstly, there was Vartos the Turk, and then Duranno the Spaniard, who was followed by Lopez his fellow countryman. He stepped forward with a jaunty and defiant air which secured him a loud tribute of applause. Leon, whose bearing was more dignified than the rest, was the last to appear.

When all was arranged, the attendant priests pressed the crucifix to the lips of the condemned men, whose faces wore an indescribably hideous aspect, with the features just dimly shadowed through their white caps.

At the moment Calcraft left the scaffold, Lopez, who had objected strenuously to the concealment of his face, made a spasmodic effort with his pinioned hands to lift the cap and take a last look at the world. His exertions almost succeeding.

Just ten minutes elapsed between the appearance of Blanco on the gallows and the fall of the drop, but it was some minutes before all the men ceased to exist. Two of them evidently died in protracted agony, the struggles of Lopez being especially violent and horrible to witness. Leon appeared to be the only one who was put instantly out of his misery.

A more awful and sickening scene had rarely been witnessed, and it sorely tried the nerves of those whose professional duties compelled them to witness many an execution. The mob, evidently scandalised and disgusted, gave vigorous vent to their feelings, and this ration of horror was greeted by their groans and exclamations.

When Calcraft mounted the scaffold on hour later to cut down the bodies, he was greeted with a torrent of hisses, counterbalanced by some very slight applause. He smiled superciliously at the crowd and, with a mirthful expression on his face, he exchanged some jest with the men who were placing the coffins ready for the bodies. To complete his task Calcraft clasped the swinging corpses, set their feet in the coffins and then cut the rope so that the bodies fell into their shrouds.

As he unhooked the ropes from the chains, the show was at an end and the crowd, laughing, hustling and bustling, dispersed to spend the day in drinking, thieving and harlotry.

In the chill morning air the hangman had finished the story of the *Flowery Land* by the sharp slamming of the drop and the agony of dislocated neck bones and choked lungs.

Within days, the verse shown opposite appeared in print.

# Mutilated Remains in Minerva Place

On a Friday afternoon in the middle of August, 1849, the neighbourhood of New Weston Street, Bermondsey, was thrown into considerable excitement in consequence of the discovery of the mutilated remains of a man in one of the houses in Minerva Place, near the new Leather Market. The house belonged to Mr. Coleman, a builder, who, about six months previously, let it to a man named Manning, a discharged railway servant and his wife.

The corpse had been discovered by Police Constable Barnes who, on searching the premises, had inspected the stone flags in the back kitchen and had found the earth between them to be soft. Removal of the flags was at once undertaken and when a lady's stocking was discovered near the surface, it was decided to dig deeper. As the earth was shovelled out, a foot was perceived protruding through the mould, and by the time they had dug to a depth of three feet they had uncovered a body, placed face down with the feet tied, or rather trussed up. The hole had been lined at the bottom with slaked lime, some of which had also apparently been thrown over the body. Where the head lay there were marks of blood, and the impression of the upper part of the body was plainly traced upon the lime. From the appearance of the pit into which the body was placed, there was little doubt that it must have taken several days to have had it in readiness.

It was revealed that the deceased was Patrick O'Connor, a ganger in the customs at the London Docks. He had been missing for eight days, and on the afternoon he disappeared he had been met by a friend near Manning's house, where he said he was going. From that time he had not been seen by any of his acquaintances, but being in the habit of leaving home for some hours, no notice was taken of his initial absence. Eventually, the hours turned to days, and when he had not returned home on the Saturday, hand bills were quickly printed and circulated, offering a reward of £10 for his discovery.

The concerned relatives and friends of Tipperary born O'Connor pointed the police in the direction of the Manning household. Mr. O'Connor had been a frequent visitor to their home in Minerva Place and his jocularity with Mrs. Manning was markedly observed by the residents who lived either side. He was almost always to be seen smoking, in the company of Mrs. Manning, at the back parlour window, and also in the small garden at the rear of the premises.

A couple of days prior to the discovery, the constable had visited the house to make inquiries respecting the missing man. Mrs. Manning had appeared to express her astonishment at his absence and seemed absorbed in grief that no tidings could be heard of him. On that occasion she stood in the back kitchen, immediately over the concealed corpse, and answered several questions as to when she last saw him, without seeming to be at all terrified.

Patrick O'Connor had been in England many years, after abandoning an intended career in the church, a profession taken up by his brother, a Roman

Catholic priest. He had the reputation of being wealthy, often cashing accommodation bills and was called 'the custom's money lender'. His salary in the customs was £170 per annum, and two days before his disappearance he took out £100 from a savings bank.

An inquest was held at the Leather Market Tavern and the room, though a large one, was crammed to inconvenience. The majority of those present were relatives and friends of the deceased. The jury viewed the body, which was still naked, as when found, and being partly covered with lime, decomposition had commenced.

Witnesses declared that they recognised the unfortunate man by the length of his chin, which was remarkably thin and projecting, and by his mouth, which was toothless, the deceased having an entire set of false teeth.

At what period of the night, or under what circumstances, the man's life was taken was the subject of various conjectures. It was inferred, from a bottle on the sideboard containing laudanum, that the deceased had been drugged, and that while he was in that state he was fired at, either with a gun or pistol. The ball had passed through the head and a surgeon's examination revealed that the skull had been beaten in with a crowbar or some other heavy instrument. It was assumed that death had ensued long before the whole of the injuries were inflicted, one fracture extending from the back of the head to the left eye.

Whether the deceased had been stripped of his clothes in the room where he was murdered, or after he got downstairs, no judgement could be formed as not a vestige of his clothes could be found. From the appearance of the copper fireplace it was supposed that all his clothes had been burned.

Statements of those in adjoining houses suggested that the murder had taken place about midnight, on Thursday the 9th of August, as one or two had been woken by a noise emanating from the lower part of the Manning's house.

The initial inquest was adjourned for a period of seven days, and it was announced that the Government was offering a reward of £100 for the apprehension of Manning and his wife, or £50 for the apprehension of either. Her Majesty's pardon was also offered to any accomplice, not being the person who fired the fatal shot, who should give such information on evidence that would lead to the conviction of the murderer. A telegraphic communication was sent along the various lines of railway and a full description of the suspected murderers was posted in nearly every town in the country.

Frederick George Manning was formerly in the service of The Great Western Railway Company as a guard, and was implicated in the extensive robberies that took place on that line. In a twelve month period over £4,000 was stolen from the trains on which he was the guard. Consequently he was discharged from the company's service.

Maria Manning, before her marriage, had been in the service of the Duchess of Sutherland's household. Her maiden name was Maria de Roux and she was born in Geneva, Switzerland. An extremely fine woman, her manner appeared those of an accomplished lady.

*Maria and Frederick George Manning fled the horror scene*

The couple's movements on the days after the murder added to the suspicion that surrounded them. Mr. Manning's first act on the following morning was to call upon a broker to dispose of their furniture. His wife was seen to leave the house early in the forenoon and did not return until the evening.

She was, in fact, traced to the lodgings of the deceased, and with the keys which must have been obtained from his pockets, she opened the drawers and took everything of value.

On the Tuesday after the killing, Mr. Manning slept at the house of the broker to whom he sold the furniture. He appeared rather agitated and anxious, and that night he sent out for a shilling's worth of brandy, which he drank up at once.

Maria Manning had shown considerable nerve, and it was said that on the Sunday she had roasted a goose over the spot where the corpse of Mr. O'Connor was lying. Her coolness had quite thrown the police off their guard. Almost immediately after their visit she ordered a cab, loaded it with three tightly packed boxes, and drove off, putting her head out of the window and instructing the driver, "Be quick, drive fast".

The realisation that they had absconded and the discovery of the body led to a great 'hue and cry' throughout the land. There were supposed sightings of them in places far and near, and one source suggested that they had taken flight on board the *Victoria*, bound for New York. The ship was carrying two passengers by the name of Manning, but they proved to be a mother and daughter.

It was only a matter of days, however, before detectives managed to trace Maria Manning to Edinburgh, where she was arrested. In her possession was found a quantity of the property of the murdered man. Among the items found were receipts for money lent by the deceased and letters from him to her, prior to her marriage, being addressed in her maiden name. Her luggage also contained various documents of property and some articles of wearing apparel that had belonged to O'Connor.

Mrs. Manning was examined immediately and, after being cautioned, her response was that she had nothing to say. Officers were despatched from Scotland Yard to convey her to London. The party left Edinburgh just before mid-day on the Caledonian Mail Train and arrived at Euston Station, London at five o'clock next morning.

She was taken to Horsemonger Lane gaol where she was attended by female turnkeys to whom she occasionally addressed observations, but none of her remarks applied to the crime with which she was accused. The scantiness of the wardrobe at her command appeared to annoy her very much.

The police continued to pursue the other suspect of the atrocious murder with unwearied industry, and intelligence came to light that he had absconded to Jersey. At once the island became the scene of intense police activity, and a tip off from a publican centred the search on St. Hellier. As a result the local chief of police and detectives from London descended on a local inn and, at ten o'clock at night, entered the room in which he was staying. Confronted by the officers, he confessed the murder and said his wife was the instigator, and she had fired the shot into O'Connor's head as he went downstairs. He also claimed that he intended to give himself up next day had he not been captured.

Towards the end of October, the Mannings stood trial and when they were placed in the dock they looked rather pale, but perfectly calm and collected. Maria Manning, aged 28, was wearing a black dress, fitting closely up to the throat, a shawl of somewhat gaudy colours in which blue predominated, and primrose coloured gloves. She was without bonnet and wore as a head-dress what appeared to be a very handsome white veil. The sixty-year-old male prisoner, described as a traveller, wore a dark suit of clothes.

The Counsel for Mrs. Manning attempted to have her tried as an alien by a jury composed half of foreigners. It was decided, however, after much debate, that as she had married a natural born subject the trial must proceed.

It was revealed that Patrick O'Connor had been a suitor of Maria de Roux before she became Mrs. Manning and that after her marriage a close intimacy was still maintained. O'Connor was a man of substance and his wealth was known to Mrs. Manning who, apparently, had made several ineffectual attempts to get money out of him.

The inference was that this fiendish woman at last made up her mind to murder him and appropriate all his possessions. It was said that she had coolly confided her intention to her husband, a heavy brutish fellow, and it was claimed on his behalf that he had been aghast at his wife's resolve and tried to dissuade her.

The evidence against both prisoners was most damning and it was no surprise when the jury delivered guilty verdicts against both parties. Mr. Justice Cresswell at once put on the black cap and the female prisoner delivered an address of some length, declaring that she was most unjustly treated and perfectly innocent. She became very passionate and excited, frequently interrupting the Judge as he passed sentence of death, holding out no hope of mercy.

On leaving the dock, Mrs. Manning threw a twig of rue into the court exclaiming, with great indignation and temper, "A shame for England". The male prisoner simply bowed to the Judges as he disappeared from view.

The trial and subsequent confession by Mr. Manning seemed to piece together the activities on the fatal day. It appeared that Mrs. Manning had induced O'Connor to go down to the kitchen to wash his hands, and that she had followed him to the basement. There she had stood behind him as he stood near the open grave she herself had dug, and which he mistook for a drain. While he was speaking to her, she put the muzzle of her pistol close to the back of his head and shot him. She had then run upstairs, told her husband, made him go down and look at her handiwork and then, as O'Connor was not quite dead, Mr. Manning had delivered the final blows with a crowbar.

Mr. Manning's demeanour was in harmony with his situation and his full confession elucidated all dark and uncertain points in connection with the crime. Mrs. Manning exuberated a full range of emotions, being furious, flippant, despairing and finally displaying reckless effrontery. She expressed the utmost contempt for her husband, mocked the chaplain and turned a deaf ear to the comforters. Through all she ate heartily at every meal, slept soundly at night and talked cheerfully on almost any subject.

Exactly three months and three days after the crime was committed, the Mannings reached their hour of destiny in front of Horsemonger Lane gaol. As the final minutes ticked away Mr. Manning requested to see his wife. They both entered the chapel and sat on the same bench, with only two watchers intervening between them. Leaning towards his wife, he said "I hope you are not going to depart this life with animosity. Will you kiss me?" She replied that she had no animosity toward him and they kissed each other.

The sacrament was then administered to them and they again kissed and embraced each other. Manning saying to his wife, "I hope we shall meet in Heaven".

At that moment the governor appeared and said that time pressed. The hangman, Calcraft, came forward, the wretched pair being conducted to different parts of the chapel to be pinioned. The male prisoner submitted to the operation with perfect resignation, but his wife's natural strength forsook her and nearly fainting, she was brought round with a tot of brandy.

The couple were then taken along a succession of narrow passages onto the gallows, which were gazed upon by a vast multitude. The male convict wore a suit of black and his wife was attired in a handsome black satin dress. Calcraft prepared the culprits in the usual business-like manner and, for a fleeting

# Farewell to Manning and His Wife

Some verses taken from a circulation by a 19th century printer:

Maria Manning came from Europe,
Brought up respectable we hear,
And Frederick Manning came from Taunton
In the County of Somersetshire.
Maria lived with noble ladies,
In ease, and splendour, and delight,
But on one sad and fateful morning,
She was made Frederick Manning's wife.

She first was courted by O'Connor,
Who was a lover most sincere,
He was possessed of wealth and riches,
And Loved Maria Roux most dear.
But she preferred her present husband,
As it appeared, and with delight,
Slighted sore Patrick O'Connor,
And was made Frederick Manning's wife.

And when O'Connor knew the story
Down his cheeks rolled floods of tears,
He beat his breast, and wept in sorrow,
Wrung his hands and tore his hair,
Maria dear how could you leave me,
Wretched you have made my life,
Tell me why you did deceive me,
For to be Frederick Manning's wife.

At length they all were reconciled,
And met together night and day,
Maria by O'Connor's riches,
Dressed in splendour fine and gay.
Though married yet she corresponded
With O'Connor all was right,
And oft he went to see Maria,
Frederick Manning's lawful wife.

At length they plann'd their friend to murder
And for his Company did crave,
The dreadful weapons they prepared
And as they fondly did caress him
They slew him - what a dreadful sight,
First they mangled, after rubbed him,
Frederick Manning and his wife.

They absconded, but were apprehended,
And for the cruel deed were tried,
When placed at the bar of Newgate,
They both the crime strongly denied,
At length the jury them convicted,
And doomed them for to leave this life,
The Judge pronounced the awful sentence,
On Frederick Manning and his wife.

Return at once to whence they brought you
From thence unto the fatal tree
And there together be suspended,
Where multitudes your fate may see,
Your hours recollect is numbered
You betrayed a friend and took his life,
For such there's not one spark of pity
As Frederick Manning and his wife.

See what numbers are approaching
The Horsemonger's fatal tree,
Full of bloom in health and vigour
What a dreadful sight to see.
Old and young pray take a warning,
Females lead a virtuous life,
Think upon that fatal morning,
Frederick Manning and his wife.

moment, their pinioned hands touched in a last farewell. The next moment the drop fell and both convicts appeared to die without a struggle.

After hanging an hour the bodies were taken down and casts taken of their heads, despite Mr. Manning's plea for this to not happen. For the sake of his family he did not want a cast of his head to be exhibited at Madame Tussaud's.

Mrs. Manning's appearance on the scaffold in a black satin dress brought the costly fabric into disrepute and its unpopularity lasted for close on thirty years.

**Postscript**

The execution scene earned the disapproval of Charles Dickens who described it thus :-

"a sight so inconceivably awful as the wickedness and levity of the immense crowd collected at the execution this morning could be imagined by no man, and presented by no heathen land under the sun. The horrors of the gibbet, and of the crime which brought the wretched murderers to it, faded in my mind before the atrocious bearing, looks, and language of the assembled spectators. When I came upon the scene at midnight the shrillness of the cries and howls that were raised from time to time, denoting that they came from a concourse of boys and girls already assembled in the best places, made my blood run cold".

# Long was the wait until Justice Called

This tale began in the year 1782 on the tiny island of Goree, off the African Coast, and ended on the gallows at Newgate Goal, almost twenty years later.

The crime that took so long to bring to justice occurred on the 10th of July, 1782. That morning the Orderly Sergeant, Edmund Lewis, was on duty at the gate of the Governor's house on Goree, when over twenty men from the garrison went by in search of the paymaster. The Governor, Joseph Wall, desired Lewis to go and ask the men what they wanted. This he did and the men stated that they were going to ask the Commissary to settle their accounts and pay them an allowance they were entitled to, in consequence of them having been on short rations.

As the Commissary was about to sail for England with Governor Wall on the next day, they wished to have their accounts settled before he departed. The Governor, on hearing this, sent word that if the men did not go back immediately to the barracks, he would order one half of them to be flogged. On receiving the message, the men all returned to their quarters in an orderly and submissive manner.

About an hour later a body of men decided to confront the Governor and headed for his house. Amongst the company was Sergeant Benjamin Armstrong who, when the Governor met them, spoke on their behalf. After the Governor had enquired of their intentions, Sgt. Armstrong had, in a respectful manner, taken off his hat and said, "Your Excellency, we want the Commissary to settle with us before he goes to England". The Governor's response was to order the men back to barracks, a command to which they submitted without any disrespectful language, disturbance or threat of mutiny.

After dinner the Governor went down to the main guard on the parade ground and began to beat one of the Guard with his sword. He then took a bayonet from a sentry and, after striking another with that, he ordered that man and the sentry to be placed in confinement. He then ordered the drummer to beat the long roll to call all the men on Parade, the garrison being told to fall in immediately without putting on their uniforms. This they obeyed and arrived without arms. The men were then formed into a circle two deep and a gun carriage was brought in to the centre.

The Governor then called Sergeant Armstrong out of the ranks, had him stripped and tied to the gun carriage. He was then flogged by half a dozen natives who inflicted the punishment in rotation at twenty five lashes a time. All the time the Governor stood in the circle and urged the natives to do their duty, calling out, "Lay it on, cut him to the heart, cut him to the liver". In all, eight hundred strokes were administered with the thick rope and, after he had received his punishment, Armstrong was taken to the hospital.

Within another four days Armstrong was to die from the beating he had taken, by which time the Governor and the Commissary had sailed for England.

Enquiries into Governor Wall's behaviour were instigated because no Court Martial had taken place and Sergeant Armstrong had been given no chance to defend himself. The result was that the Governor was ordered for trial in 1784 but, as he was being escorted to London for that purpose, he fled his escort.

For the next eighteen years he lived on the continent, mainly in France and Italy, and then, perhaps thinking his crime long forgotten, he returned to England. By this time most of those who had been under his command in the garrison were dead, but the authorities felt capable of gaining a conviction.

Amongst those called to the Old Bailey to testify against the former Governor of Goree were the Orderly Sergeant, Edmund Lewis, who was by this time a Bow Street officer, and the garrison surgeon, Ferrick. The trial took place on the 20th of January, 1802 before the Lord Chief Baron, Mr. Justice Lawrence.

The surgeon told how, when the circle had been formed, he had been called for, and when he arrived Armstrong was being flogged. The Governor had told him that Armstrong was an infamous scoundrel and being duly punished. In his opinion, the surgeon was sure that the flogging, which had been severe, was the cause of death. Sergeant Lewis gave a very detailed account of the incidents on

*Former Governor Joseph Wall spent his final days in fervent prayer*

the day of the flogging and remarked that he had never before seen a soldier punished with such ferocity.

Governor Wall's version of events was that a mutiny had taken place and he claimed that he had obtained the unanimous support of his fellow officers to punish the ring leaders. His account of events centred on the fact that he had conducted a Regimental Court Martial and that Captain Lacy, who was new dead, had told him that the sentence of this body was one of 800 lashes for Sergeant Armstrong.

The jury had, firstly, to decide whether or not a mutiny had taken place and, secondly, whether the punishment was in proportion to the offence. They took forty five minutes to reach a guilty verdict.

The Recorder told those gathered that no man, however high his situation, however great his power, should be at liberty to dispose of the life of a fellow creature. He hoped that God would forgive Governor Wall his sins and then the sentence of death was passed in the usual manner. The proceedings had begun at nine o'clock in the morning and closed at eleven o'clock that night, with the prisoner leaving the dock with a look of resignation on his face.

A week after the sentencing a council was held at St. James's to consider the case and the verdict was that the law should take its course. Governor Wall had not entertained any hope of a respite and he was duly informed that execution would take place the following morning. From the time of conviction he had not partaken of any food and was in an emaciated condition. A forlorn figure, he spent his time in fervent prayer as he awaited the final punishment for a crime he had committed in middle age.

Joseph Wall appeared on the scaffold at eight o'clock in the morning. The 65-year-old former Governor was dressed in a grey mixed coat with a black collar and dark pantaloons, and in his hand he held a handkerchief.

The immense crowd that had gathered gave three cheers as soon as the executioner began to place the halter around the neck of the unhappy man. He did not remain above two minutes on the platform before the drop fell, but he was a considerable time in dying, during which he was much convulsed. The handkerchief which he held in his hand to drop as a signal, was kept in his grasp until the executioner removed it half an hour later.

Left to lament his departure were his wife, who came from a very respectable family, and a son of nine years age. On being cut down the body was placed in a cart to go for dissection, but the Surgeons Society displayed a little humanity by handing over the body to his relatives.

# A Shocking Chelsea Suicide Shooting

On the 9th of August, 1872, Auguste Dirks, a waiter and native of Hannover in Germany, was aboard the steamer from Ostend to Dover. On board the vessel he came into conversation with two young Germans, Paul Julius May and Herman Nagel. The young men told Dirks that they also came from Hannover and that they were on their way to America. At the time Dirks was living at Dover, and the pair of them asked him to accompany them to London, to act as their interpreter.

On the day they arrived in London the three of them, and a German couple, went shopping in Oxford Street. Besides the usual purchases of clothing and novelties, a gun was bought by Nagel, who paid £2 for the six-chambered revolver complete with cartridges. Nagel telling his companions that he needed to protect himself from pickpockets.

On the Sunday that followed the group spent the day in Hyde Park, and the day after they visited the Crystal Palace and the Surrey Gardens. At the latter place both May and Nagel practised with the revolver, and they finished their day's sightseeing by going to Cremorne Gardens. In the refreshment room of that place they made the acquaintance of three girls, one of whom was a German woman, Augusta Burgess, who had been in England about ten years. They remained in the gardens about half an hour, and before leaving they made arrangements to go to the girls lodgings in Langton Street, Chelsea the following day. This they did and, in fact, remained there the whole night – May associating with Burgess in the front room on the ground floor, Nagel spending his time with Ellen Gordon in the back room and Dirks enjoying the company of Elizabeth Curtis in a first floor room.

On the Wednesday the three young men went about together spending money and visited several places, including Euston Square Station. Whilst there May and Nagel told Dirks they intended going to America. After collecting their luggage, the pair of them booked on a train for Liverpool and Dirks bade them farewell.

To the surprise of Augusta Burgess the two young Germans turned up at her Langton Street rooms on the Friday morning. Pleased to see them, the woman was happy to allow May to share her room again and Nagel was welcomed into the arms of Ellen Gordon.

The reunions, however, were not without their problems and the women noticed that on a number of occasions the men were quarrelling about some matter of apparent importance. Burgess also became concerned when a number of items of clothing and jewellery went missing and she began to believe that the pair were short of money and that they had visited the pawnshop to obtain cash for such things as her shawl, their watches and chains, and the overcoats which they had arrived in. To add to her worry, the men still had in their possession the revolver they had purchased and May, in particular, seemed anxious that it remained with him.

On the following Wednesday the two men went out for the day, returning about six o'clock and appearing to be in good spirits. Shortly afterwards Miss Burgess went out to Cremorne Gardens, leaving May, Nagel, Ellen Gordon and Elizabeth Curtis in the house.

After Burgess had left, the other three sat together in the ground floor apartment. After a while May wrote a note and handed it to Nagel who, after reading it, said "Ja, Ja". Shortly after, Ellen Gordon went to her room and remained there a little while. When she came to go back downstairs, she met Nagel on the landing and he asked her if he and his companion could use her room for a few minutes. It was a request she agreed to, going down to the ground floor to occupy herself.

Not long afterwards Elizabeth Curtis, who was in the drawing room on the ground floor, heard two reports of a pistol and a stumbling noise from the room above. She at once ran for Gordon and the servant, and when the locked door was forced open a tragedy was before their eyes. Nagel was lying on the sofa, blood flowing from his mouth and breast, and May was lying with his head under the table, and with his feet touching the sofa. Both had obviously been shot, and by the side of May was a revolver.

Nagel was quite dead. His waistcoat and shirt were unbuttoned and there was a wound to his left breast. May was still alive and he also had suffered a wound to the left breast, through his shirt, which appeared scorched. Aid was soon on hand and May was given brandy and water, but little hope was held out for his recovery.

As the police searched the house for clues to the tragedy, a letter was discovered on a chest of drawers in Augusta Burgess's room. It was written in German and addressed to Miss Burgess. When translated it read as follows:

"We separate today from thee. The cause is this. We have fled from Berlin in order to escape from military service. We took our cash, 2,000 thalers, with us, and this sum is now gone. Relations I have none. For that reason we do it. Thou lyest too much to my heart. I cry for thee from my heart and for thy fate. Good bye. We shall not see each other any more. Perhaps we may in the other world. For me the world is nothing any more. Good bye, or follow me, dear. I should have done it before this time; love to thee has kept me back. The watch is thine; fetch it, in fact everything else. Once more, a hearty good bye. From thy lover, PAUL MAY".

On the reverse side, written across, was the following instruction:

"Take the pawn tickets in your possession and redeem what you may desire to have.
Thy friend.
Herman Nagel, from Germany".

Two days later the police obtained what they believed would be a dying deposition from May. In it he claimed that Nagel had shot him and then turned the pistol upon himself. The bullet was still in May's body and must have passed close to the heart, but as the days passed he appeared to grow stronger, being eventually removed to St. George's hospital.

In fact, by Thursday, 21st November, 1872, he was deemed fit enough to stand trial at the Central Criminal Court before Mr. Justice Grove, accused of the murder of his fellow countryman. Auguste Dirks, who had befriended the Germans on their arrival in the country, and the women from the Langton Street lodgings were amongst the witnesses called to relate the events that led to the shootings.

Inspector Gill of the constabulary told how he had found the bodies after being alerted to the incident, and he reported that examination of the revolver revealed that three of the chambers were loaded, two had been recently fired and the sixth one had not been loaded.

The divisional surgeon told of his visit to the scene of the incident and expressed the opinion that the shirt of Nagel had been pulled aside by his left hand, and that he had used his right hand to shoot the revolver at himself.

When Mr. Justice Groves summed up the case he reminded the court that the prisoner was a foreigner, unacquainted with the English language and the English law. He pointed out that if the two men had gone to the room for the purpose of suicide, each abetting and encouraging the other by acts or words, then if one survived he would be guilty of murder no matter by whose hand the mortal wound was inflicted. He then went on to say that if, however, Nagel met his death by his own independent act, and the prisoner was in no way privy to it, and if afterwards the prisoner shot himself, he would not be guilty of murder. He concluded by stating that if there was any reasonable doubt, the prisoner was entitled to the benefit of it.

The proceedings had lasted twelve hours, but the jury took only fifteen minutes to return with a 'Not Guilty' verdict. Paul Julius May, just 21 years of age and with a boyish appearance, smiled broadly as the verdict was delivered. The hour was late when the trial ended and at the suggestion of his Counsel, the young man decided to remain in Newgate gaol for the night and taste freedom at the dawn of a new day.

**Postscript**

In February, 1873, it was reported that Paul May had been convicted for forgery in Berlin.

# Park Lane Killing of Madame Riel

Amongst the residents of Park Lane, London in 1872, was the 46 year old Madame Marie Caroline Besson Riel who lived with her daughter in a household that was maintained by a couple of servants and a cook.

The mistress and her daughter were of French origin and early in 1872 Madame Riel, who was known to be quick tempered, employed a Belgian woman, Marguerite Diblane, who was 29 years old and unmarried, to replace an outgoing domestic servant. The new servant could speak little English, but was able to converse with the others in French. She did not, however, prove to be satisfactory in her employment and the daughter, Mademoiselle Riel, told her, towards the end of March, that she wished her to leave. The Belgian woman insisted that she was entitled to a month's notice or month's pay and, somewhat reluctantly, Mlle. Riel allowed her to work out her notice at the Park Lane residence.

On the last day of March, Mlle. Riel left London for Pari. When she returned home, early in the morning of Monday, the 8th April, she was greeted by the other servant, Eliza Watts. The servant was in an anxious state telling Mlle. Riel that her mistress, Madame Riel, had gone out on the Sunday morning at about eleven o'clock to walk in Green Park and had not returned. She also reported that Marguerite Diblane had left the house the previous evening.

Mlle. Riel then looked about the house to see if mamma had left a note for her. Her search ended in the pantry, which was always kept locked because it contained a safe. On opening the pantry door, she saw her mother's body lying on the floor with her cloak draped over her. A rope was round her neck, with a slip noose under the left cheek. Part of the rope was twisted twice round the handle of the safe door, and the other end was hanging loose over the body.

Within minutes, 13 Park Lane was the scene of great excitement as police and medical assistance rushed to the house. A doctor was soon examining the body of Madame Riel and his conclusion was that the woman had either been strangled by a rope or throttled by hand, and that a couple of severe bruises on the face were not the cause of death.

Suspicion immediately fell upon the absent Marguerite Diblane and a cab driver came forward to reveal that on the Sunday evening a woman who spoke broken English had boarded his cab, asking him to drive to Victoria Station. A clerk at the station later revealed that the woman had boarded a train bound for Paris at nine o'clock that night. She had paid for her ticket with a five pound note, receiving two sovereigns in change. At least £30 had gone missing from the safe in the pantry and it was felt some of this money had funded her journey.

The police search for Marguerite Diblane was to end in Paris a few days later. Upon being apprehended a portemonaie was found in her possession containing rings and bank notes which had been taken from Madame Riel's safe.

When asked to explain her crime, the woman claimed that her mistress had become angry because preparations for dinner had not commenced and grossly insulted her. Madame Riel had then grabbed her by the throat and, as violent words passed between them, she gave her mistress a sudden blow, from which she fell dead.

It appeared Madame Riel had gone down to the kitchen at about eleven thirty that morning and, after the killing, the servant had dragged the body into the coal cellar to conceal it from the housemaid, Eliza Watts. Soon after, Diblane sent the housemaid out for some beer and on her return kept her waiting some time at the house door. During that interval she had dragged the body into the pantry, where it was found the next morning.

The trial of Marguerite Diblane took place in mid June, 1872 at the Central Criminal Court before Baron Channell. The main facts of the case were simple and admitted on both sides. Her Counsel endeavoured to show that the crime was reducible to manslaughter, but on the decisive advice of the Judge, this possibility was ruled out.

Witnesses were called by the Defence Counsel to testify as to Madame Riel's behaviour towards her servants. It was said that she had been a very passionate person, often ruled by her temper. By nature she was of a very suspicious disposition and sometimes blamed persons unjustly. When excited, she gesticulated a great deal and would throw up her hands and throw her head back.

There was nothing to disprove the prisoner's account of the provocation she received, and the belief was that the act had not been premeditated. The facts appeared to suggest a sudden quarrel, a mistress slain in the heat of argument and, in panic, a robbery and a flight to Paris.

The trial ended with Marguerite Diblane being found guilty of murder with the jury making a strong recommendation to mercy. A French Inspector of Police had told the prisoner that if she had been tried in France, extenuating circumstances would have been taken into account. Baron Channell, however, acted upon the guilty verdict and informed the woman that she would be executed for her crime.

The jury's feelings were made known to the Home Secretary and a week later the Belgian emigrant was informed that the death sentence had been commuted to one of penal servitude for life.

# Covent Garden Theatre
# Reduced to Ashes

On the first Tuesday evening in March, 1856 the Covent Garden Theatre in London was filled for a *Bal Masque,* under the management of Professor Anderson, the so called wizard of the north.

The theatre kept up the entertainments with the vigour which generally characterised such recreations. Many of the dancers left between two and three in the morning, others remained much later; and by five o'clock not more than two hundred persons were left assembled in front of the orchestra. The last dance was completed and Mr. Anderson, observing the flagging spirits of his guests, gave the signal to his Master of Ceremonies to close the revels with the usual finale of *God save the Queen.*

At this moment a man who was engaged in conversation with Castle, the fireman, observed a bright light shining through the chinks and crevices of the flooring in the carpenter's shop, high overhead. In an instant both of them left the stage and hastened towards the point of danger. Neither their departure nor their errand had been observed, and the crowd below them still kept up the chorus to the music of the National Anthem.

The carpenter's shop extended from one end of the building to the other, and lay between the ornamental ceiling and roof of the theatre. Through an open space in the floor of the workshop, the central chandelier was lighted. When the two men entered the place they were nearly suffocated by dense black smoke. Castle threw himself on his hands and knees and endeavoured to crawl towards a smouldering heap near the centre of the workshop. The smoke was, however, too much for him and he was compelled to make a hasty retreat without having been able to open the fire mains on that floor. Descending to the next 'flies', he succeeded in turning on the mains, but before he could fix the hose the fire falling from the workshop above overtook him.

The imminent peril was now evident to him and he realised the fire had taken a mastery which could not be controlled. His next step was to cut away those parts of the scenery most likely to be affected by the increased fire. The orchestra had not ceased playing the National Anthem when the sudden fall onto the stage of one of the beams, around which the scenery was rolled, gave the first intimation of the danger to those assembled below.

Mr. Anderson was the first to give the alarm of "Fire!" and the terror and tumult caused by this announcement can easily be imagined. The remaining masquers rushed precipitately to the various exits – of which the police had taken immediate possession. Thus they were able to rescue from the selfish alarm of many of the stronger sex, their terror stricken partners. Several women were, in fact, trampled on and a number were carried out fainting, but none were seriously injured.

There was something hideous in this sudden change from mad revelry to ghastly fear. Already the rush of air towards the roof had fanned the fire in to brighter life and fiercer energy. Wreaths of white smoke began to curl from the stage into the body of the theatre. The musicians leapt from their seats and fled, in many cases without even saving their cherished instruments. The interior of the theatre was almost immediately cleared of the visitors.

The flames rushed forward and whirling round the interior, made it at once their own. The ballet girls and minor characters of the masque came flying from their dressing rooms into the passages of the theatre and, in many instances with difficulty, they were led to safety by the police.

Officers were positioned on the doors and they prevented the excited multitude that gathered from forcing their way madly in to the burning house. The proceeds of the night, which lay in the treasury, were rescued from danger, and certain valuable documents and papers were rescued from the secretary's office.

In the few minutes that had elapsed, the doom of the theatre had been sealed. The flames had burst through the roof, sending columns of fire high up into the air, which threw in to bright reflection every tower and spire within the circuit of the metropolis. The whole fabric of St. Paul's was brilliantly illuminated and a flood of light was thrown across Waterloo Bridge.

The glare acted as a speedy messenger in bringing up the fire engines, which now proceeded from every quarter of London. There was no want of water, but neither engines nor water were of any avail in saving the property. The theatre blazed like a furnace within its four hollow walls and, at half past five that morning, the roof fell in with a tremendous crash. Showers of fiery sparks and burning charcoal were thrown up and then poured down onto the streets, which were crowded with onlookers.

The danger to houses surrounding and facing the theatre attracted the efforts of the firemen. In Bow Street, the Royal Italian Opera Hotel and the adjoining houses were almost on fire several times and it required the constant application of water to cool their blistered fronts. The Plaza, Tavistock and Bedford Hotels all suffered damage from the fire, but fortunately the efforts of the fire brigade preserved the surround properties.

Whilst attempting to salvage some valuables from the theatre a policeman was surprised to see a man at one of the windows over looking the courtyard. He had been asleep and not even the raging of the fire, nor the shouts of the people had awakened him. He had only stirred when the room had become full of smoke and breathing had become difficult. A ladder was brought at once and he was rescued from his perilous position.

Nothing remained of the theatre but the skeleton and ruined walls. All the scenery, props, wardrobes and dramatic library had been consumed by the raging inferno. In fact, barely anything was spared, even four original paintings by Hogarth, representing the 'Seasons', had been destroyed.

It was rumoured that two persons were missing and fears were entertained for their safety. One was a boy employed by the gas man and it was feared he had

*Despite the efforts of the fire crews, the blaze engulfed the theatre*

fallen asleep in some quiet corner of the theatre. The other was a Miss Hamilton, known to have been present at the entertainment but not seen since the outbreak of the blaze. Fortunately, they both turned up later in the day at homes of relatives and great relief was felt that no human life had perished in the fire.

By six o'clock a telegram had been sent to Mr. Gye, the lessee of the building and he immediately returned from Paris to view the devastation. The theatre had been let to Mr. Anderson for a few weeks for a season of pantomime and the termination of the loan was the masked ball – an event Mr. Gye had originally vetoed.

In the course of the day several members of the nobility and aristocracy visited the doomed theatre and even a visit was made by Queen Victoria and Prince Albert.

It was stated that the building itself was uninsured and the loss to the proprietors, who held a large number of shares, quite terrible. The precautions against fire had been most stringent and four firemen had been employed to guard the theatre against fire. It was felt that the fire must have been smouldering for some considerable time, but the origin remained a mystery.

## Postscript

Two years after the blaze a new building was completed and the theatre was once again ready to entertain. The original theatre, in Covent Garden, of harlequinade notoriety, was opened in December, 1732, and rebuilt in 1792. That building was burnt to the ground in September, 1808. On that occasion, twenty two lives had been lost by the fall of the burning roof. The rebuilt theatre was opened in September, 1809, and was said to have cost £150,000 to erect. In 1846 the building had been entirely remodelled and converted in to an Opera House, reopening in April, 1847. Superb operatic performances over a number of years had earned the theatre a place amongst the highest ranked in Europe.

# Insane Attack upon His Majesty

In the year 1830, King George IV died without an heir and his brother William took up the throne. William was a bluff, hearty sailor who was popular, although not fully respected.

During the month of June in 1832, as was the custom, William IV and his Queen Adelaide attended the horse racing at Ascot Heath. On the Thursday of the race meeting, His Majesty, accompanied by his Consort, had just reached the grandstand and advanced to the front window to acknowledge the respectful greetings of his people, when an attack was made. Two stones were hurled in His Majesty's direction in quick succession. The first stone rebounded from the building on to the ground below, and the second stone entered the open window and struck the King a blow on the front of the head.

An instant alarm was raised and a thousand arms were extended to seize the individual who had made the attack. His Majesty was much agitated and retired to the inner part of the room, apparently in alarm lest further violence should be attempted. His main concern was for the safety of Her Majesty and the ladies who made up her entourage.

Fortunately, due to the fact that the stone had struck His Majesty's hat, he had received only a slight injury. In fact, the Royal party appeared perfectly reassured long before the alarm of those present had subsided.

The wretched author of the mischief had been immediately secured and was taken at once before the Chief Magistrate of Westminster. He was questioned in a makeshift court room beneath the grandstand. In a few moments the room where the examination took place was crowded with people anxious to learn details of the act and to view the King's assailant.

The accused gave his name as Dennis Collins, and wore the tattered garb of a sailor. He was an elderly man with a wooden leg, and looked as if he had received some rough treatment from the mob before he had reached the custody of the police officers. He chose to make no statement before the Magistrate and was eventually committed to Reading Gaol for later examination.

The next interrogation took place the following Wednesday. On that day witnesses to the incident were called and

*It was an eventful day at the races for King William IV*

their depositions taken. Collins then addressed the Magistrates in his own defence in the following manner:

"I own myself at great fault for throwing these stones at His Majesty. I was in Greenwich Hospital on the 16th of December last, as an in-pensioner. I had been there eighteen months. The ward-keeper was sweeping the place. I told him he had no business to sweep it more than once a day; the boatswain's mate abused me, and I returned it. A complaint was then made to the Governor and I was expelled for life.

I petitioned to the Lords of the Admiralty to have the pension which I had before I went into hospital restored to me. I am entitled to that pension by an Act passed in the reign of King George IV, which entitles a pensioner to have the same pension which he had before he became an in-pensioner, unless he struck an officer, or committed felony, or did anything of the kind, which I did no such thing.

On the 19th of last April I petitioned the King to have my pension restored. He answered me by sending the petition to the Lords of the Admiralty and Mr. Barrow, the Secretary, sent a letter to me at a public house, the 'Admiral Duncan', with the same answer the King gave. The answer was that His Majesty could do nothing for me. This was partly in writing and partly in print. I had neither workhouse nor overseer to apply to, and had not broken my fast for three days; mere distress drove me to it.

His Majesty never did me an injury and I am exceedingly sorry I threw a stone or anything else at His Majesty. On the 17th of the present month I went to Admiral Rowley's; he swore at me and kicked me. I can only say I am sorry for what I have done and must suffer the law. They had no right to take my pension from me, to which I was entitled by Act of Parliament".

After the statement was heard Collins was fully committed to trial in the customary fashion, upon a charge of High Treason.

The trial took place at Abingdon on the fourth Wednesday of August in 1832. When brought into court the accused laughed aloud, and nodded and kissed his hand to several ladies in the room. The prisoner was charged with the highest crime against the law, in attempting the life of his Sovereign. The learned Counsel remarking that it had only been due to the fact that the King's hat intercepted the blow, that His Majesty's life had been saved.

The examination and the confession of the prisoner were read and two Counsel addressed the court on behalf of the prisoner. They contended that he had been excited and, in fact was a mad man. They also claimed that he had been drinking prior to the incident, having been given a shilling the day before by a gentleman.

The evidence complete, the Learned Judge then told the jury it was sufficient to prove the intent. The jury, in ten minutes, found Collins guilty of throwing the stone with intent to do His Majesty some bodily harm.

Collins was then allowed to address the court, but his statement was rambling and not intelligible. Considerable excitement was then produced in court as the Judges put on their black caps. The greater portion of the spectators were quite unprepared for such a termination of the trial.

Justice Bosanquet, as the senior Judge, then addressed the prisoner, concluding with the following words:

"The sentence of the court is that you be drawn on a hurdle to the place of execution where you are to be hanged by the neck until you are dead; your head is then to be severed from your body, which is to be divided into quarters, and to be disposed of as His Majesty thinks fit".

Thus ended the trial. From the expression of the Judge in passing sentence, however, it was believed that a pardon would be granted in view of the circumstances surrounding the crime.

On the following Friday a respite was received and the sentence was eventually commuted to transportation for life. Collins was sent from this country to Van Diemen's land and a short residence in that colony ended his days. Aged over seventy, he died at Port Philip in the spring of 1834.

## Postscript

King William IV died in June 1837. His reign had included the Reform Bill of 1832, which gave political status to the middle classes, the new Poor Law of 1834, the abolition of slavery in British Colonies of 1833, and the Factory Act to improve working conditions, also passed in 1833.

# Killing Time in Kentish Town

A crime took place in London, in the year 1890, that was to be long remembered for its singular brutality, accompanied by a great deal of cunning.

The victims of the atrocity were 31-year-old Phoebe Hogg and her infant child, Phoebe Hanslope Hogg, the sole offspring of her short marriage to haulier Frank Hogg. The couple had married in November, 1888, setting up home in Prince of Wales Road, Camden Town.

For a period of five years Hogg had been acquainted with another woman, known by the name of Mary Eleanor Pearcey. Though she was unmarried, the 24-year-old had taken the name of a former lover in preference to her maiden name of Wheeler.

After his marriage Frank Hogg had continued to make regular visits to Mrs. Pearcey's home in Priory Street, using a latch key to gain admission. Until Christmas 1889 the two women were unacquainted, but that festive season saw the husband introduce the women to each other.

Following that meeting Mrs. Pearcey became a frequent visitor to the Hogg household. So much so that when Mrs. Hogg fell ill, her new acquaintance was happy to nurse her back to health.

Shortly afterwards husband and wife quarrelled and a short separation ensued, although they were soon reconciled and living again together. This reconciliation, however, did not curtail Mr. Hogg's visits to Priory Street, where his relationship with Mrs. Pearcey had developed into an intimate one.

Passion had begun to run deep in the bosom of his mistress, and by the autumn she had the desire that he should belong to her alone. To this end on Friday, 24th October, 1890, the mistress had a letter delivered to the Hogg's home, inviting the wife to visit in the afternoon. Mrs. Hogg was pleased to accept the invitation and by three o'clock, with the child in the perambulator, she set off for Priory Street.

Her husband was completely oblivious to the afternoon's happenings, having left for work before nine o'clock that morning. When he returned home, some twelve hours later, he was surprised to find mother and child absent. Since his wife's father had been critically ill, he assumed that she had been called to his home in the country at short notice. He retired that night with the resolve that next morning he would himself make the journey to his wife's father.

That evening there was a great outcry in Hampstead when the body of a woman was discovered. The corpse was observed under a wall, near the junction of Adamson Road and Eton Avenue. The victim's head was almost severed from the trunk and was immersed in a pool of blood. A little later, some half a mile distant, a blood-stained and empty perambulator was found in Hamilton Terrace.

The police at once came to the conclusion that the perambulator had been used to convey the body from the scene of the killing to Hampstead. To complete the evening's grisly discovery, the body of a child was found in a field in Finchley Road. The infant appeared to have died either from suffocation from smothering or from exposure to cold.

Early the next morning Clare Hogg, the sister-in-law of Phoebe Hogg, visited Mrs. Pearcey to enquire about the missing mother and child. Mrs. Pearcey at first denied seeing them, but afterwards admitted that Mrs. Hogg had visited her that afternoon, saying that she had called for the purpose of borrowing money, a circumstance which she did not wish her husband to know about.

Once the identities of the victims had been ascertained, and Frank Hogg had returned from his fruitless trip to his wife's father, he was informed of the tragedy. Volunteers were required to visit the mortuary to identify the corpses and Clare Hogg and Mrs. Pearcey volunteered

*Mary Eleanor Pearcey was accused of murder*

to carry out the task. Whilst there Mrs. Pearcey exhibited behaviour that excited suspicion and, aware of the victims visit to Priory Street, the police resolved to visit the lodging house.

Inside the premises they observed signs of a fearful struggle with the walls, doors and various articles of furniture bespattered with blood. Blood was also found on Mrs. Pearcey's clothes, her hands were cut and scratched, and an attempt had been made to saturate the bloodstains with water and paraffin so as to destroy the evidence.

The police were convinced that Mrs. Pearcey was the perpetrator of the crime and she was formally arrested and charged. On the day of the killings Mr. Hogg had worked continuously and there were no grounds for believing he was in any way connected with the circumstances of the crime.

A long chain of evidence seemed to connect Mrs. Pearcey with the foul deed. The motive being her desire to claim the husband of her victim. Both the committal and trial aroused much interest and although she protested her innocence, the accumulated testimony suggested otherwise.

The body of Mrs. Hogg had been discovered wrapped in a cardigan jacket which was later identified as his, by the man Pearcey, with whom the accused had previously co-habited. On the fateful afternoon Mrs. Hogg had been seen standing outside the lodging house in Priory Street. In the evening other witnesses had spotted Mrs. Pearcey wheeling a heavy looking perambulator in the direction of

Hampstead. A tenant of the lodging house recalled the crashing of glass and the cries of a child in pain.

All this and more led to the inevitable guilty verdict, and nine weeks after the crime Mrs. Pearcey awaited execution. Attempts were made to gain a reprieve on the grounds of insanity, the Home Secretary deciding not to interfere with the sentence and to allow the law to take its course.

The execution was set for the morning before Christmas Eve in 1890. On that Tuesday, despite a bitter frost and slippery streets, small knots of people commenced gathering outside the Old Bailey.

The executioner, James Berry, had arrived at Newgate gaol a couple of days prior to the occasion, and when he observed Mrs. Pearcey through the Judas hole in the door of the condemned cell to judge her weight and build, she told one of the wardresses that he was in good time.

At a quarter to eight on the appointed morning the bell of St. Sepulchre's Church on the viaduct began ringing out sharply in the morning air. The solemn tolling of the culprit's funeral bell had little effect on the crowd, many of whom were women. Obscene and ribald jokes could be heard amongst every group, the females especially being fierce in denouncing the prisoner's conduct. It being apparent that not the slightest sympathy was felt for her by the members of her own sex.

That morning Mrs. Pearcey had been awakened shortly before six o'clock by a female warder and soon after had been joined by the chaplain. At ten minutes to eight she was removed to the pinioning room where Berry adjusted the leather throngs around her arms. She submitted quietly, though was somewhat dazed. Her drawn features and pale skin reflected the suffering she had undergone.

She walked steadily to the small shed in the gaol yard where the execution was to take place and was placed on the fatal drop. The noose was deftly placed over her head, the lower bolts were drawn back and she disappeared from view as the drop fell. A slight swinging of the rope and all was over, death being practically instantaneous.

As the black flag was raised, the waiting crowd gave vent to their feelings with a loud cheer.

Later that morning it was revealed that the woman had, after prayers in her cell, made a full confession, stating to the chaplain, "The sentence is just, but the evidence was false".

# The Arsonist's Atrocity in Oxford Street

During the summer days of 1832, the residents of London's Oxford Street set about their business early, and the last Monday in May was no exception.

On that morning, shortly before six o'clock, Henry Oddell was just about to open his master's shop when he heard a cry of "Fire" from the opposite side of the street. He immediately looked across the way and saw a man attempting to escape from the grating of 398 Oxford Street, the home of Jonathan Smithers. Oddell ran across the street and, realising that it was Mr. Smithers beneath the grating, attempted to raise it as the trapped man pleaded, "For God's sake get me out! The house is on fire".

Unsuccessful in his attempt, Oddell then rushed back into the thoroughfare and alerted a couple of constables who hurried to the scene. By this time the shop premises on the ground floor, which were occupied by a printer, were ablaze, and after forcing the front door, the police officers were unable to descend to the basement kitchen where the flames trapped Smithers.

Having realised that there would be no escape through the grating, Smithers was forced to retreat through the kitchen. Making his way up the blazing stairs, he was successful in reaching the ground floor and, in fear for his life, he dashed through the flames that engulfed the shop and reached the safety of the street. His dash from danger left him much burned about the face and hands and his clothes were alight as testimony to the spread of the fire. The sudden admission of air through the shop door served to increase the fury of the flames and soon the whole of the lower part of the premises were ablaze.

Jonathan Smithers was at once dispatched to the Middlesex Hospital for his wounds to be dressed, and attention switched towards the other occupants of the premises. At almost every window people in peril were observed, bewailing their sorry plight and imploring aid with uplifted arms.

A servant girl spotted at a third floor window indicated that she would throw herself into the street, but those gathered entreated her to descend to a lower level before she made so hazardous a leap. When she next appeared, at a second floor window, a group of men placed themselves under the window to catch her upon descent. With great courage she found the strength of mind to throw herself out and landed safely in the arms of one of those below. The man was knocked over and considerably hurt, but the girl walked away unharmed.

Alas, not all had the girl's good fortune. On the second floor of the house lived the Twamley family. When they became aware of the danger all hopes of escape by the staircase had vanished, and they ran from window to window in a state of distraction.

Occupying their rooms at the time were seventy-year-old Mrs. Twamley, her two daughters, Eliza and Caroline, and their nephew, Napoleon Farengo, who was an orphan.

Eliza Twamley was spotted at a window with her eleven-year-old nephew in her arms. She appeared more alarmed for his safety than her own and hesitated as she contemplated the necessity to jump. Eventually, the flames caught hold of her clothes and the boy fell out of her clutches and down to the street. Eliza fell prey to the flames and the boy landed head first on the ground, dying shortly afterwards.

Meanwhile drama was surrounding the other daughter, Caroline, who was attempting to save her aged and bedridden mother, who suffered from chronic asthma. Endeavouring to rescue her mother, she had seized her in her arms and carried her from the bed through to a ledge outside one of the first floor rear windows. The pair of them were spotted by neighbours and a ladder was immediately brought and placed against the wall. Unfortunately, before assistance could be given, the pair of them dropped to the ground below. The women had been engulfed by fright and the fall left Mrs. Twamley mortally wounded, and her daughter seriously injured. The elderly woman died some two hours after and the daughter was made comfortable in her injured state.

On the following day a Coroner's Inquest was held on the body of Eliza Twamley who had been a fine young woman and a dancer at Covent Garden Theatre. In the course of the inquiry it was revealed that the authorities believed the fire had been wilfully started.

Suspicion of guilt fell upon Jonathan Smithers, and it was stated that the fire had started at the bottom of the kitchen stairs, where the remains of burnt shavings were distinctly perceptible. In the back vaults, next to the kitchen, a trail of gunpower had been discovered, leading to another sack of shavings. The trail of powder had not ignited and remained as evidence of an intended act of incendiarism. In consequence the Coroner's jury recorded a verdict of wilful murder against Mr. Smithers.

Further inquests on the boy and Mrs. Twamley came to the conclusion that Napoleon Farengo's death was the responsibility of Mr. Smithers, and that the elderly woman had died of fright.

Two weeks later it was decided that Mr. Smithers was sufficiently recovered from his injuries to be removed to Newgate gaol from the Middlesex Hospital, where he had been treated.

On the first Friday in July, 1832, he was tried at the Old Bailey accused of the 'Wilful Murder' of Eliza Twamley and Napoleon Farengo. Whilst the indictments were being read, the prisoner shed tears and concealed his face with an handkerchief. The prosecution stated that a person committing an illegal act, by which human life is sacrificed, is equally guilty of murder as if he had committed it with his own hand.

Sarah Smith, a servant to Jonathan Smithers' household, told the court that she had observed her master with the sacks of shavings and in possession of bottles which contained turpentine. She had gone to bed just before midnight on the Sunday before the fire, and at that time the fires in the parlour and kitchen stoves he been extinguished. On being alarmed by the cries of "Fire" early next morning, she had thrown open a first floor window and jumped to safety.

The court was told that a policy of insurance existed between Smithers and the British Fire Office for £700, and this was suggested as a motive for the diabolical crime.

In his defence the prisoner read a lengthy statement claiming that the fire had been started by accident and that, in an attempt to stop the progress of flames, he had been severely injured himself. He claimed that the blaze had left him reduced to poverty, not believing that he was entitled to anything from the policy of insurance. He concluded by throwing himself on the mercy of the jury. He then called several respectable witnesses who gave him an excellent character for good conduct and humanity.

The learned Judge began his summing up at eleven o'clock at night and finished his address three and a half hours later! He was frequently interrupted by the prisoner who was anxious to explain particular circumstances in connection with the evidence.

The jury spent half an hour deliberating their verdict and returned into court at three o'clock in the morning to announce a 'Guilty' verdict. The Recorder immediately pronounced that the prisoner would be hanged on Monday next and his body delivered to the surgeons for dissection.

Smithers heard the verdict with much composure and, gathering up his papers, was led from the dock.

On the Saturday afternoon his wife and children were permitted to take their final leave of him and their visit lasted a couple of hours. That night he tacitly acknowledged that he had fired the house, and expressed himself unfortunate to be the first to suffer under the new Act of Parliament which made him answerable for the death of anyone who fell victim to the flames of an arsonist.

His last night was a restless one, and at twenty minutes before eight on the Monday morning the execution party arrived. He walked to the gallows with a firm step and took his place under the beam with similar fortitude. After a last gaze at the vast crowd who had assembled to witness his end, the cap was drawn over his face. After the rope had been adjusted, the drop fell, and in a moment he ceased to exist. After being suspended for an hour the body was cut down and delivered to St. Bartholomew's Hospital for dissection.

# Assassination of
# Prime Minister Perceval

At the beginning of the nineteenth century a man named John Bellingham was engaged in mercantile concerns in Liverpool. He was in a prosperous situation, and in the year 1804 he went to Russia on some trading business of importance to him.

At that time a ship called the "Soleure" was lost in the White Sea. She was chartered for England and, by the directions of her owners, insured at Lloyd's Coffee House. The underwriters at Lloyd's refused to pay the owners for the loss and the decision was received with indignation.

As things transpired, Mr. Bellingham, who had no connection whatsoever with the disputed vessel, was about to embark on his journey home when the news from Lloyd's was received. The intelligence incurred the wrath of the Russian authorities and, as an act of reprisal, the Military Governor of Archangel ordered that Mr. Bellingham be seized in his carriage as he was passing the Russian frontier. He was thrown into prison from where he sought the assistance of the British Ambassador, Lord Granville Leveson Gower.

The British Ambassador immediately demanded the release of the prisoner, but the Governor responded by claiming that Mr Bellingham had been detained for a legal cause and that he had conducted himself in a very indecorous manner. The response of the Russian authorities was enough to cool the British Consul's interest and despite the prisoner's attempts to induce the British authorities to interfere, he was detained in durance for almost two years.

At length, however, after being handed from prison to prison, fed on bread and water, treated with the utmost cruelty, and frequently marched through the streets under military guard, he was allowed to make his case known through the Procureur. It was investigated and Mr. Bellingham obtained a judgement against the Military Governor and the Senate.

Notwithstanding this verdict, he was immediately sent to another prison, and a demand was made on him for 2,000 rubles. It was alleged that the payment was owed to a Russian merchant who had, in the interim, been declared bankrupt. Claiming the debt was a false one, Bellingham refused to pay and was declared a bankrupt. The custom in Russia at the time was that any foreigner so declared was automatically detained for three months for all Russian creditors to make their claims, and a further eighteen months for creditors world-wide to come forward.

Although the Senate sent forth clerks to enquire of all strangers who arrived whether they had any demands against Mr. Bellingham, none were forthcoming. Despite this he was still passed from gaol to gaol and the 2,000 rubles demanded of him. Lord Gower refused to interfere in the business and the prisoner, although not destitute of the means of payment, resisted the claim on account of its gross injustice. He felt that payment would in some way justify the conduct of the Senate and the Military Governor of Archangel, against whom he had already obtained a legal decision. Refusing to comply with the Russian authorities request he remained in prison while his young wife of twenty years of age, who had been residing in St. Petersburg, set off for England.

Lord Gower continued to refuse to represent his case to the Russian Emperor and for five years Mr. Bellingham languished in confinement. Eventually in 1809 he received a discharge from prison and was issued with an order to quit the Russian dominions immediately.

On his return to England he laid a statement of his grievances before the Marquis Wellesley, claiming redress for the injustice inflicted upon him due to the conduct of the British Ambassador in Russia. The noble Marquis referred the matter to the Privy Council, and they passed it on to the Treasury; and thus it was bandied from one department to another.

He was next advised to petition Parliament and he drew up a petition in the hope that sufficient members would support him. The reception he received was a cool one and he was referred to the Prime Minister, Spencer Perceval, who at the time was also carrying out the duties of the Chancellor of the Exchequer. The Treasury had informed Mr. Bellingham that as his claim was partly of a pecuniary nature he would require the sanction of Mr. Perceval.

When Mr. Perceval had familiarised himself with the claims of the petitioner, he applied the principles of justice which always guided his conduct, and refused Mr. Bellingham his countenance.

From this point Mr. Bellingham found himself bereft of all hope of redress, his affairs had been ruined by his long imprisonment in Russia, his family driven into tribulation and want. Feeling that justice had been refused to him by the Government, he could no longer conceal his resentment of those in high office.

He remained in London and, filled with the desire for revenge, he spent some considerable time planning an act of retribution. The target of his attention became Mr. Perceval, who had been Prime Minister since 1809, and who was the figurehead who had dismissed Mr. Bellingham's claims after he had spent over two years attempting to obtain the justice he sought.

A brace of pistols were bought, along with the ammunition, and an alteration was made to his dress coat by the addition of an inside pocket on the left side for containing his pistols. For a number of weeks he was a familiar figure in the vicinity of the House of Commons and he familiarised himself with Mr. Perceval's movements. He was determined to elude the possibility of prevention of his intended action, and on Monday the 11th of May, 1812, he placed himself at the entrance of the lobby and awaited the arrival of the victim of his malignity.

Shortly after five o'clock that afternoon, Mr. Perceval made his appearance in the lobby. Before he could advance he was confronted by his would-be assassin, who drew out a small pistol and shot the Prime Minister in the lower part of the left breast. Mr. Perceval moved forward a few faltering steps and, when halfway

*John Bellingham*

up the lobby and about to fall, some persons stepped forward and caught him.

He was immediately carried to the room of the Speaker's secretary and the surgeon was sent for. On examining the wound, the medical man observed that the ball had entered the heart and the Prime Minister's condition was beyond assistance. Less than a quarter of an hour after receiving the fatal wound he was dead, and amongst those who witnessed his passing was his brother, Lord Arden, who had rushed to the scene.

The deed had been perpetrated in a moment and a person who was behind the victim seized the pistol from the hand of the assassin, who retired towards a bench and surrendered himself without any resistance. All the doors of the House were locked and he was taken to one of the apartments called the prison room. On searching Bellingham, another pistol was found in his pocket and when an official asked him if he was the villain who shot the Prime Minister, he replied, "I am the unhappy man".

Bellingham was then subjected to an examination, which continued for some time, and during it he preserved an air of perfect calm. Various witnesses were called and when proceedings terminated, he was committed to Newgate gaol for trial.

As the evening wore on, the crowds outside the main entrance were swelled by a concourse of pickpockets and those of the lower orders. When the mob surrounded the hackney-coach intended for transporting the prisoner to Newgate, it was thought advisable to find another route and exit was made by the Speaker's entrance.

On the following Friday before a packed Old Bailey, the 42-year-old father of three, John Bellingham, stood trial for the murder of the Right Hon. Spencer Perceval. When asked to plead he complained about the hurry with which the trial was taking place and in a subdued tone of voice, he said "Not guilty. I put myself upon God and my country".

The proceedings recalled the accused man's confinement in Russia, his attempts to obtain redress for his imprisonment and the cold-blooded killing of the Prime Minister.

When called upon to explain his actions, the accused told how he was driven to despair, stating that Mr. Perceval was the victim of his desperate resolution.

*The assassination of Prime Minister Perceval*

He concluded by disclaiming most solemnly all personal or premeditated malice against Mr. Perceval. As to death, he stated, if it were to be suffered five hundred times he would prefer it to the injuries and indignities which he had experienced in Russia.

In the latter stages of the day long trial the state of mind of the accused was scrutinised. One woman claimed he had spent all his life in a state of derangement, and another thought he had acted strangely since his return to England. Cross-examination of the witnesses emphasised that no medical records of insanity existed in regards to the prisoner, and a picture of a man in full control of his own affairs was drawn by the prosecution.

When His Lordship addressed the jury, he impressed on them the importance of putting out of their minds entirely all considerations of the high character of the lamented gentleman who had been killed, pointing out that the laws of he country hold out their protection equally to the humblest and the highest subjects of the state.

The twelve men retired for only a short time and when they returned they had with them a guilty verdict. The prisoner was reminded of the enormity of his crime and informed that he would be executed on Monday morning next, and his body delivered for dissection.

The funeral of Mr. Perceval took place the following morning and was conducted in as private a manner as was consistent with the circumstances. The deceased's widow wished to avoid any stately appearances on the melancholy occasion. Mr. Perceval's body, in a hearse drawn by six horses, was taken from Downing Street to the churchyard at Charlton and, after the service, was deposited in the family vaults of Earls of Egmont. The coffin of the father of twelve, who was the second son of the late Lord Egmont, had a plate fastened to it with the following inscription:

"Right Honourable SPENCER PERCEVAL
Chancellor of the Exchequer, First Lord of the Treasury, Prime Minister
of England fell by the hand of an assassin in the Commons House on
May 11th, A.D. 1812, in the 50th year of his age, born Nov. 1st A.D. 1762"

On a wet Monday morning a large crowd assembled to witness the execution of John Bellingham. At seven thirty he was brought down from the cells at the Old Bailey to have his irons knocked off. He was dressed, as at his trial, in a brown great-coat, a striped kerseymere waistcoat, light pantaloons and shoes that were down at the heel.

By eight o'clock he had been prepared by the executioner and the attendant clergyman, and was standing on the scaffold facing an irreverent mob. After the cap had been placed over his head and the rope around his neck, a perfect silence ensued. The supports of the scaffold were struck away, Bellingham sank and, after a slight struggle, the executioner, who was below, began pulling his legs so that he may die quickly.

The body hung until nine o'clock and once it had been cut down it was placed in a cart and covered with a sack. The body was then conveyed up to the Old Bailey, along Newgate Street. The populace followed the cart closely and the executioner two or three times removed the sack from the body so that it might be seen. The cart's journey ended at St. Bartholomew's Hospital in Bell-Yard, where the body was delivered.

To the end, Bellingham had steadfastly refused to express contrition for his crime, or Mr. Perceval's fate, and he firmly denied having had any accomplices in carrying out his diabolical deed.

# The Gallows
# and the Hammersmith Ghost

During the final month of 1803 and the opening days of 1804, the people who resided in the vicinity of Hammersmith became somewhat perturbed by the belief that a ghost was nightly haunting the neighbourhood. Sightings of the phantom were commonplace and idle chatter led to the belief that a figure dressed in white stalked the highways and by-ways.

Dependant on who was telling the tale, the ghostly apparition had horns, glass eyes and other features guaranteed to send a shiver down the spine.

Concern was heightened in mid-December when news spread of the death of a woman after a frightening experience. It was reported that the woman had been passing the local churchyard at ten o'clock at night when she had seen a very tall, white figure rise from amongst the tombstones. Struck with fear she had attempted to flee, but the apparent phantom had overtaken her and pressed her into it's arms.

At that point she had fainted, remaining in a collapsed state until discovered by some passers-by hours later. After relating her experience to her rescuers, she was taken home and put to bed. Her terrifying ordeal having a tragic end because after lingering a few hours in her bed, she passed away.

Her death served to highlight the fears growing in the community. Many believed it was the apparition of a man who had cut his throat in the neighbourhood some twelve months before, whilst others believed that a prankster was at play. Such was the concern that a number of young men resolved that they would lay in wait for the ghost. In consequence, each evening the by-ways and footpaths were patrolled by those eager to solve the mystery. There were many sightings during the nights that followed, but always the ghostly figure fled into the dark.

Amongst those who encountered it was William Girdler, the watchman of Hammersmith. When he saw the figure it appeared to him to be draped in either a white sheet or a large table cloth. Keen to unravel the mystery he had gone in pursuit and before it disappeared into the distance, he had observed that it appeared to gather its flowing garment up on to its shoulders.

The watchman's experience had occurred on the last Thursday in December, 1803 and five days later, as the ghost hunting continued, tragedy was again set to befall the neighbourhood.

On that fateful Tuesday evening, Thomas Milward, a journeyman bricklayer, who resided with his in-laws in Hammersmith, visited the nearby home of his parents. It was about ten o'clock when he arrived at the family home, and for a few minutes he talked with his parents and his sister about the domestic problems he was encountering in the home of his wife's parents.

After hearing the watchman pass by and call out the half hour, he bade his mother, father and sister goodnight and set off for the short walk home. His sister lingered at the door as he departed and within a minute she heard a shout of, "Tell me who you are, otherwise I will shoot you". Within seconds a gun was fired, and in the distance she saw her brother slump to the ground. Her parents heard the news in disbelief and hurrying to the spot, Ann Milward was faced with the lifeless body of her brother.

The watchman, William Girdler, was soon upon the scene and after viewing the body, he went to the 'White Hart' public house in Hammersmith where Francis Smith was waiting to tell Girdler of the tragic deed he had committed. Smith was in an agitated state and he told those gathered that he had called out twice and after receiving no reply, had fired his pistol.

Girdler had spoken to Smith earlier in the evening and he had told the watchman that he was out ghost hunting. Smith was adamant that he had believed he was in confrontation with the alleged phantom due to the dress of the deceased, who had unfortunately been in his working clothes, which consisted of long white trousers and a white waistcoat.

Whatever the intent of the 29 year old Francis Smith, the authorities thought fit to bring him to trial, and on Friday the 13th of January he was brought before the jury in the Old Bailey, accused of the 'Wilful Murder' of Thomas Milward just ten days earlier.

When he was placed in the dock he was dressed in a suit of black, and the pallid hue of his countenance and the outward signs of his contrition seemed to command the sympathy of every spectator.

A surgeon by the name of Flowers testified that he had examined the body of the deceased and found that he had died from a gunshot wound in the lower part of the left jaw. The shot had disfigured the jaw and the face was all blackened with the powder from the gun.

Amongst those who related the facts of the case were the watchman, William Girdler, and the victim's sister, Ann Milward. Pheobe Foulbrook, the mother-in-law of the dead man, was also called. She informed those gathered that Thomas Milward had told her that, on the Saturday evening prior to his death, he had been mistaken for the ghost, with a gentleman and two ladies being frightened as he walked along the terrace. On hearing his tale, she had advised him to wear a great coat of an evening to avoid any further misunderstanding.

A brewery servant, Thomas Groom, who resided in Hammersmith was also called, and he told of a night just before Christmas when he and a fellow servant had been hurrying through the churchyard. He claimed he had met the ghost and it had laid hold of him by the chin and that when he had put forth his hand, it had disappeared into the night.

After his Lordship had recapitulated the whole of the evidence, the jury retired. They returned a little over an hour later to announce a verdict of 'Guilty' of manslaughter. On hearing this, His Lordship was adamant that such a judgement could not be given, and he told the jury they must either find a verdict of murder or acquit the prisoner.

After reconsidering the evidence and the words from the bench, the jury returned for a second time to announce that they found Francis Smith 'Guilty' as charged. Upon a call for silence His Lordship then proceeded to pass the sentence of death telling Francis Smith that, "The law of God and man is, that whosoever sheddeth man's blood shall atone for his offence by his own".

The verdict and the sentence stunned the prisoner, and after being told he was to be executed on Monday next, he was unable to walk back to his prison cell without the assistance of two of the prison wardens.

The outcome of the trial was immediately reported to the authorities and so speedy was the response that by seven o'clock that night Francis Smith was informed that he had received a respite during His Majesty's Pleasure. Two weeks later he was told that a pardon would be granted after him being imprisoned for one year.

# Calamity at the Christmas Pantomime

During the middle of the nineteenth century, the popularity of the Christmas pantomime led theatre managers throughout London to provide productions which proved very lucrative, and were very well attended by the humbler classes, especially, the young of either sex.

To take advantage of this situation, a pantomime was arranged for Boxing Day, 1858, at the Victoria Theatre in the generally poor district of Lambeth. The theatre was situated at the intersection of Waterloo Road and the New Cut, in the centre of a densely populated area. In anticipation of the show's popularity, two performances were scheduled. The first commencing at half-past one o'clock in the afternoon, and the second starting at half past six o'clock in the evening.

In order to prevent any confusion or accident arising from the departure of the afternoon visitors and the influx of those wishing to view the evening performance, the theatre manager introduced a special entry and exit procedure.

It was arranged that the people in the gallery at the first performance should, instead of leaving the theatre by the ordinary staircase, descend through a lobby leading to the boxes and go out by the principal entrance. The manager's object in making these arrangements was two fold; to avoid any collision between the ascending and descending people, and, at the same time, enable the gallery doors to be thrown open at an early time, so as to prevent a crush at the entrance.

The doors were thrown open at one o'clock for the afternoon performance and the theatre was, as expected, almost immediately crammed. Everything went well throughout the performance and laughter and gaiety echoed through the auditorium.

As that performance was drawing to its conclusion, the stairs leading to the gallery, which were of wood and contained several landing places, were becoming packed with those awaiting the evening's entertainment. With each minute the crowd increased, but they were barred from entering the theatre by locked doors at the top of the gallery staircase.

Despite the crush on the staircase, it appeared that all was going to plan until some of the waiting crowd became aware of a strong smell of gas. No alarm was at first felt, but when a slight explosion took place on the third landing of the staircase a fearful cry of "Fire! Fire!" led to a scene of horror.

The whole mass of people on the upper reaches of the staircase, where the explosion took place, at once attempted to descend. To add to the danger those on the lower levels of the staircase continued to ascend, unaware of the panic from above. The outcome was that more than a hundred people became tightly wedged in the middle of the staircase. This terrible situation lasted for upwards of fifteen minutes, and when the pressure of the crowd relented there lay a dense, sickening and motionless mass of bodies on one of the landings.

The police had been alerted quickly and a large body of constables were soon at the theatre. A heart-rending scene followed as the officers removed the bodies from the staircase into the street, amidst groans and shrieks from those outside the premises as they recognised the lifeless corpse of a friend or relation.

The police secured the services of all the passing cabs and vehicles and sent off those with injuries to the hospital. In a short time over twenty medical men were busily examining the dead and insensible, and soon a degree of calm had been restored.

When the full extent of the calamity was known, it was found that sixteen persons had lost their lives and upwards of thirty people had been injured.

Although so frightful an occurrence had taken place on the stairs of the gallery, the great mass of people in the theatre had been blissfully unaware of the fight for life so near to hand.

The inquest into the tragedy took place on the following Thursday, with the bodies lying at the Lambeth Workhouse. The proceedings terminated in a verdict of "Accidental Death", and with a recommendation being made that in future sufficient time should be allowed for clearing the theatre of the first audience before the evening visitors were admitted.

The manager, Mr. Johnson Towers, told the hearing that in his opinion the calamity had been greatly increased by the gas piping being disturbed by those people anxious to escape. He, of course, regretted the unfortunate loss of life that had ensued.

# Innocent Victims of Red Lion Square

On the second Wednesday in August, 1865, the neighbourhood of Red Lion Square, Holborn was thrown into a state of great excitement when news spread of an appalling atrocity that had taken place at the Star Coffee House and Hotel in Red Lion Street.

The train of events had begun on the previous Saturday when a respectably dressed man had called at the hotel and enquired if three children could be accommodated with a bed for a few nights. He told the proprietor of the hotel that they were about to embark for Australia within the following week. He was informed that one room would be available and, after inspecting it, agreed it would suit his purpose.

As agreed, the man arrived on the Monday evening with the three boys and saw them to bed. The next morning the children were downstairs by half past six and in a cheerful mood. They stayed in the coffee room until the man who had brought them returned at about eight o'clock. After breakfast the man left, but he returned at mid-day when the children dined. Again he departed, saying he would see them in the evening.

The man arrived back at the hotel at six o'clock and the children partook of tea, bread and butter. He then said that as they might be tiresome, he would take them to bed. Firstly, however, he asked if another room could be provided. This was agreed by the proprietor and the man put the children to bed. The two younger boys, aged six and eight years, being placed in the same room as the previous night, and the eldest child, a ten year old, occupying the newly appointed chamber.

The man then went out, saying he would shortly be back, and he made his appearance at nine o'clock. He asked for a candle to see that the children were settled and after remaining upstairs a short time he left the hotel, stating he would return in the morning.

He did not, however, make his appearance and, as the children had been downstairs early the previous morning, some doubt existed as to whether they should be awakened. When half past eight arrived and still the youngsters had not stirred, one of the chambermaids was instructed to awaken them. Entering the room of the two younger children, she approached their bed to discover, to her horror, that they were lying not in slumber, but in death.

The chambermaid immediately raised the alarm and the proprietor and others entered the room in which the eldest child had been placed, only to find that he also was in the sleep of death.

Medical and police assistance were immediately summoned, and the surgeon, being first at the scene, examined the bodies and pronounced that life had been extinct some hours, the limbs being perfectly rigid and cold. The appearance of the bodies suggested that they had expired without much, if any, struggling.

The police set enquiries in progress and had soon issued a description of the man who had brought the children to the hotel. He was described as about 5 feet 7 inches tall, with dark hair and a dark complexion. His eyes were said to be dark grey and although he had no whiskers, he was said to have a beard of a few days' growth.

A young lad who worked in the hotel, waiting on the tables, had been in conversation with the eldest victim and was able to provide some information. The boy had told him that the person who brought them to the hotel was not their father and that their father believed them dead. They had, the lad observed, been playing with unconcern and childish chatter right up to the time they had been taken to their beds of death.

Eventually, it was ascertained that their father was a schoolmaster named White, who was living in greatly reduced circumstances, having been separated from his wife for some considerable time.

His wife was known as the woman who had, some time since, intruded herself upon the Earl of Dudley and afterward charged that nobleman with assaulting her. The assault was said to have been committed in the noble Earl's house, where Mrs. White had gone with a begging petition. The money was for a man named Ernest Southey, a billiard marker who, she stated at the time, was "more than her husband", and had been her saviour from starvation after she had been deserted by the Earl of Dudley's brother at Brighton. In the journals of the time a long statement by Southey was published. He referred to the wrongs and the sufferings of Mrs. White, who he claimed to have rescued from an erring husband and a life of shame.

When the separation from her husband had taken place, Mrs. White had been granted custody of the children, but afterwards they returned to their father's care. Subsequently, with the consent of the father, the youngsters were given up again to the mother, and it was understood that she and her paramour were to take them to Australia to start a new life.

The Home Office were quick to react to the tragedy of Red Lion Street and by midnight bills had been posted at the police stations and other prominent places, offering a reward of £100 for the apprehension of Ernest Southey. Leading detectives were assigned to the case every railway station and other likely place was carefully watched. Southey had earned a reputation as a compulsive gambler on rowing events and horse races, and enquiries were made amongst the betting fraternity.

On the following day the unfortunate children were named as Henry White, aged ten, Thomas White, aged eight and Alexander White, aged six. Their bodies still lay at the Star Hotel and Coffee House, in the same beds in which they had met their deaths. The two younger children were placed together on an iron bedstead in a back room on the fifth floor and they had a singularly placid look, appearing as though they were simply sleeping. The eldest, Henry, had met his death in the front room and his countenance showed the same expression of repose as those of his younger brothers. On the dressing table near him lay a crumpled silk neck cloth which seemed to have been used to wipe up a little fluid. Beside the neck cloth was a small bottle which had contained the poison used to deprive the children of life.

The children had not been in good physical condition, indeed, the body of Thomas was almost emaciated. All three had been handsome and intelligent looking, their fair complexions and auburn hair giving them an innocent and joyous appearance. Their clothes, though neat, had been shabby and old, and on the bed of the eldest lay his little scotch cap, which he had evidently thrown there before getting into bed. In that boy's room the sum of four pennies lay on the table near the end of the bed and next to the coins was a bible.

The fact that the bottle containing poison had been found in Henry's room it was suggested that the two younger children had been poisoned first, and that the killer had then completed the diabolical crime by getting the eldest boy to drink the remainder of the drug.

On the following afternoon a telegram was received at Scotland Yard from the police at Ramsgate. The message revealed that Ernest Southey was in custody there on a charge of having murdered a woman and a child. It subsequently transpired that the unfortunate woman was Mrs. White, with whom the prisoner had been living, and that the child was the sister of the three boys poisoned in London.

Investigations revealed that the last place in which Mrs. White and Southey had cohabited together was at Putney, from which place the woman had fled leaving her paramour ignorant as to her whereabouts. Southey had been greatly

*Old Scotland Yard, where a telegram revealed the whereabouts of the wanted man*

distracted by the woman's actions and, in consequence, had resolved to kill the children. It was believed that after this murderous work on the Tuesday, he had proceeded directly to Ramsgate and, on successfully finding the woman, he had, in a fit of fury, put an end to her existence and that of the child.

That Ernest Southey had committed the murders there was no doubt and at his subsequent trial his guilt was confirmed. There was a plea on the grounds of insanity, the argument being that no man in his senses could have committed such an enormous crime. The Home Secretary was petitioned to spare the life of the condemned man but he did no more than his duty in allowing the law to take its course.

Southey's execution took place during the second week in January, 1866, and the feeling was that his fate was a just reward for his diabolical crime.

# Appalling Incident upon the Regent Park Ice

The cold weather and icy conditions that prevailed during early January in 1867 led to an increase in the popular pastime of ice skating. For many in London there was no better place to pursue the activity than the ornamental lake in Regent's Park. The frozen water attracted several thousand people each day and the second Tuesday of the month was no exception.

Although the ice was beginning to thaw, a countless throng skated across the lake on the forenoon. By mid afternoon the ice had begun to show unmistakable signs of breaking up, being cracked to such an extent that there was not a sound place of more than a foot or so broad. The cracks being clearly marked by the water that rose through them. The alarming symptoms were noticed by everyone and many who had sense enough departed the ice, expressing the opinion that it would not last much longer.

Despite the warnings over three hundred persons remained on the lake, skating and sliding. Shortly before four o'clock, a group of three children and two men went through the ice about twelve feet from the south-western shore. A gentleman bystander, who observed their plight, immediately plunged into the lake and brought to shore the three children, who clung around so as almost to drown him. One of the men who had fallen in scrambled out on to the ice and the other man was picked up by a boat launched by the Royal Humane Society.

Immediately after this several other people fell into the chilly water, but were soon rescued. Somewhat awakened to their position by these accidents and the shouts of the people on the banks, a few others left the ice. In most cases they, too, fell through the ice when near the shore. At this time a dozen people on the north-eastern side, near the boat-house, were standing close together, watching the misfortunes of the others, when they next fell. This was witnessed from all parts and created a panic among all those remaining on the ice who, with one accord, rushed towards the opposite shore.

As the frightened groups made for the banks, the whole field of ice gave two or three heaves and then broke up over the whole of the broad part of the lake. In an instant some two hundred adults and children were thrown into the water and a fearful cry of dismay was heard as they fell.

Those who lined the banks in their thousands shouted in horror, and all was confusion and distraction. There, in the water, could be seen children of tender years clinging to the edges of the broken ice, crying every moment in frantic voice for the assistance which those who witnessed their sufferings were powerless to render them. In a brief time their short lives were ended with a few last faint waves of the hands before the water claimed them.

The bystanders who witnessed these scenes cried and shrieked with even greater feeling than the sufferers themselves. Many relatives of those who fell in the water saw the struggles of their loved ones from the bank, yet had no possibility of saving them.

The first shock over, men rushed wildly about, seizing upon everything in the shape of a rope or spar to throw to the struggling and drowning. By this time, however, all direct communication with those in the water was cut off by the general breaking up of the ice in that area, and very few were reached. A cry was raised to get the boats and hundreds of willing workers ran off and returned with the vessels on their shoulders. When they got them into the water, the greatest difficulty was experienced in forcing them through the ice.

Ropes were rapidly joined and then, one end of each being carried across the bridge, they were stretched from shore to shore and dragged along. A few people managed to grasp them, but they could not be dragged ashore and had to remain holding on to the rope until the boats picked them up. Some of them failed to hold on long enough and the spectators were horrified to see, every now and then, a person thoroughly exhausted, relax their hold and sink into the icy water.

Many instances of individual gallantry took place. One man, at great risk, plunged into the lake and brought several children safely to shore. A man named Moore was very active and saved several persons, and a young man earned praise for diving into the lake from a rescue boat and saving a drowning man.

Within half an hour of the breaking of the ice, large bodies of police began to arrive and rendered great assistance in dragging ropes that had been caught by some of those in the water, in fetching and launching boats, and keeping idlers back.

All this time the excitement was kept up by the frequent sinking of those who had lost all power to support themselves. In some directions only splashes indicated where a human being had disappeared. Here and there a hatless head would emerge, revealing the agonised features of one who clutched at the broken slippery ice and again sank. Men were seen leaping from block to block, falling at length upon a piece large enough to sustain them for a moment, but small enough to tilt over before they had secured a place of refuge.

Nearer the banks, in the shallow water, men and women floundered about with terror stricken children in their arms. A few, by their own exertions, reached safety after being immersed in the lake for a long time. While many men shouted and wept, and women wrung their hands as they joined in the general bewailing, dozens of silent persons were plunging into the water and bringing the helpless to the shores. Those spectators who did not venture into the lake, tried hard in the main to encourage those who did, offering in some cases large rewards for the safety of a relative or friend.

A man, apparently a mechanic, was shrieking for help about fifty yards out when his cries attracted the attention of a gentleman in the crowd. Without a moment's hesitation he sprang into the water, battered a passage through the ice with his fist and made for the sinking man who immediately threw his arms round his rescuers neck and locked him in a perilous embrace. To the horror of those

*In moments, two hundred adults and children fell into the ice-cold lake*

watching both disappeared below the water line, but they ultimately returned safe to the cheers of the bystanders.

Soon darkness fell and the search for the living had to end. As the sun sank below the horizon, the weeping of women and children, who lingered on the margin of the water, heightened the gloom which this sad event had thrown over the close of a fine winter's day. Only ten bodies had been recovered amidst the attempt to preserve life and preparation to commence the recovery of the remaining bodies at daybreak were soon in hand.

The scene in Regent's Park on the Wednesday morning was a harrowing one. The public were strictly prohibited from entering the enclosure and among the thousands congregated around the park railings many a tale of woe was narrated. Anxious mothers were inquiring about missing children; relatives and friends were on the melancholy errand; and wives were crying frantically, some making eager inquiries as to their absent husbands.

The moment daybreak arrived, employees of The Royal Humane Society, all of the park keepers and a number of volunteers commenced breaking the ice, to afford the opportunity of dragging for the bodies supposed to be underneath.

*Dragging the lake for the dead* (The Illustrated London News)

During the day twenty three bodies were found, bringing the total to thirty three, in all, with the belief that others still remained to be found.

The London papers were full of accounts of the tragedy and typical of these was one by a Mr. Dunton of Hampstead who wrote as follows:

"As some wonder has been expressed at my two little ones being saved from the shocking calamity in Regent's Park, perhaps my account of the accident may interest your readers.

I was just making my way to shore, holding them by the hand, when the ice broke. One of them was a little girl of seven years of age, and the other a boy of eleven. We were then about 70 yards from the bank. Without a second's warning the ice seemed to glide from under us, leaving us in water quite five feet deep. The two little ones sank to the bottom, but rose again directly. I made a grasp at each of them, and was able to seize them by the shoulders, at the same time holding on to the ice with my left hand.

When I had them thus far safe I had time to look round. Such a sight I hope never to see again. Quite 150 persons were struggling for life. Heads and arms were to be seen all around amongst the broken masses of ice. Two yards from me a little boy was drowning, and I could not render him any help; presently nothing but his cap was visible above water. He floated in this way for some time.

I stood in this position for nearly half an hour, sinking down in the mud deeper every minute until the water reached my chin. I felt my legs being cramped with cold. I said to the eldest, "Is there any help coming, Fred? Wave my walking stick, for I am sinking down in the mud". Presently the boy said, "Father, a man is swimming to us and we shall be saved".

On looking round I saw a brave young fellow plunging through the ice towards me. The youngest child would not let go her hold of me at first; but ultimately I got her on this young man's back. He swam off with her to a boat that was now making its way towards us. When the boat came near enough I helped the boy in, and seized the side of the skiff, fearing that if I got in that it might go over with me. I held on in this manner till we got to the bank. Numbers of them had sunk out of sight long before. I tender my grateful thanks to those persons who rendered me assistance".

One incident recorded concerned a large black Newfoundland dog which had accompanied it's master on the ice and managed to get back to shore, although it's owner perished. Since the Tuesday afternoon it had refused to quit its ground despite the police attempting to drive it away. In fact, one kindly police sergeant had on three occasions offered food to the dog, but the distressed animal had refused.

The Marylebone Workhouse had been used to accommodate the bodies of the dead, and a constant stream of people visited to identify relatives and friends. The inquest into the tragedy was formally opened on the Wednesday evening and a list of victims was published.

The majority of those dead were under thirty years of age and many teenagers had perished on the tragic afternoon. In fact, the death toll was to rise to forty by the end of the week and at the resumed inquest on the following Monday, their names were added to the official list.

Various witnesses told the inquest of their experiences on the afternoon of the tragedy, including Alfred Ward who was employed as an ice-breaker. He told the gathering that he had cautioned people off the ice, but they would not go. Recalling that he had told one irate gentleman, "For God's sake get off, or there will be a calamity". He was of the opinion that the sun had had a great effect upon the ice and that the playing of hockey and the jumping of skaters had caused a great strain on the ice. He stated that an accident had occurred to three girls earlier in the day, and he had then kept his boat in the broad water to prevent the people from skating towards the part of the lake where the danger was the greatest.

Mr. Young, the secretary of The Royal Humane Society, told the inquest that he had ten men and a boy in the park at the time of the accident. In his opinion the Society's men had done all they could and three of them had been very ill after their life saving exertions.

That weekend divers were employed in Regent's Park to make a final search for bodies. The result of their investigations showed the care with which the lake had been swept by the drags, not a single body being recovered by the divers. The divers described the bottom of the lake as being composed of soft, yielding, black mud into which they had sometimes sank up to their knees. Using the latest equipment the divers had been able to stay beneath the surface for up to twenty five minutes.

In spite of the terrible accident, the lovers of skating and other sport on the ice continued to assemble daily in great numbers on the Serpentine in Hyde Park, and the lakes in Kensington Gardens, St. James's Park and Battersea Park.

A week after the tragedy skaters, had returned to the ice in Regent's Park, to the areas not disturbed by the accident, with over two thousand venturing on to the Serpentine Lake to skate by torch light until late in the evening.

# Pistol Shots in Finsbury Park

Just before noon on Friday, 22nd October, 1880, John Bradley, a railway agent of Chatterton Road, near Finsbury Park, entered the park from the Blackstock Road. A man and a woman entered about the same time and went to the inner circle. Mr. Bradley walked around the perimeter of the park and, as he did so, he observed the couple sat side by side near the lake, deep in conversation. Just as he was about to leave the park he heard the report of a pistol and, turning around, he saw the woman running away from the man who ran after her and fired again.

As Bradley dashed to the woman's aid he saw the man grab hold of her with his left hand and fire his pistol once more, this time into her breast. The woman at once fell upon her knees and held her hands up in an imploring manner. The man responded by firing another bullet towards the woman's breast, and she then slumped forward on her face.

Bradley was not alone in being alerted by the pistol shots. As he and several others approached the man, he threw his overcoat aside and pointing the pistol at his own chest, he fired. He then reeled for a short distance before falling to the ground. The man then raised himself and, with the pistol in his hand, he walked over to where the woman lay slumped. No one dared to venture too close to the pistol wielding man. By good fortune the man suddenly stumbled, and one of the anxious onlookers was alert enough to grab the pistol which had fallen from his grasp.

Bradley was then able to assist the woman. She was bleeding as he lifted her from the ground. Other bystanders crowded around the man, and he was forcibly held until a police constable arrived to investigate the commotion. It was apparent that life was fast ebbing away from the woman and she was immediately placed in a cab, which headed for the Great Northern Hospital. Unfortunately, before the cab reached the hospital the woman had died.

As the man was taken into custody he told the constable, "I shan't run away, as I have shot myself and am fast bleeding to death". He then opened his coat and showed the officer a burnt part of his waistcoat and his wound, from which blood trickled. Plans were then made to take the man to the Royal Free Hospital. In the cab he tried to grab the pistol from a constable's possession saying, "Give it me, so that I may finish the job".

After the man had been made comfortable in the hospital he was informed that the woman had died. From the articles in his possession, which included a bottle of laudanum and a photograph of the deceased, it was learnt that he was called William Herbert and that the victim was Jane Messenger, the 35-year-old wife of a business man.

Later that day, Herbert made the following statement:

"There was a certain object I had in view. I wanted to speak to her about it. I took a tram car to Finsbury Park for that purpose with the full intention of doing what I have done if the interview with her was not satisfactory to me. The reason of my doing so, no one on this living earth shall ever know".

The police immediately began to investigate the circumstances that had led to the shootings in the middle of the day in a public park. Enquiries showed that the 44-year-old William Herbert had arrived in England from Australia in the month of March, and at first had stayed with his brother-in-law, Henry James Messenger and his wife Jane, at their home in Edward Square, Islington. In the middle of August, Jane Messenger had left her husband and, along with her brother and William Herbert, had gone into lodgings in Stanley Street, Notting Hill.

The keeper of the lodging house, Sarah Deboo, told the police that the three of them, along with a child, had appeared on good terms although William Herbert had a strange manner. She related to the police how the woman, Jane

*On the day, before his death, William Herbert attended the traditional condemned sermon held in Newgate Gaol*

Messenger, had told her she had found a bottle of laudanum in William Herbert's pocket and that after she had thrown it away he had been very excitable.

The questioning of Henry James Messenger led to the knowledge that Herbert was the husband of his wife's eldest sister who lived in Foot's Cray, Australia. He had been in poverty in that country and had come to England to try and get an estate from the brother of Jane Messenger, whom he thought was dead. On his arrival here, however, he had learnt the man was still alive and his dreams of inheriting the Stockwell Park estate with its revenue of £175,000 per annum, had been thwarted.

Further enquiries suggested that Henry James Messenger had treated his wife cruelly, and a week before she had left home she had considered getting the protection of a Magistrate. On the day before her death Jane Messenger had returned to the family home, and she was still there when her husband left for work the following morning. On hearing of his wife's death, he did not rush to her, but carried on with his work, going to the mortuary the next morning.

It appeared that the woman had been happy to flee from her husband's rough treatment of her, to be protected by her brother at the Notting Hill lodging house.

Whilst in the hospital William Herbert appeared to be suffering from a great depression and seemed to care little about his self-inflicted wound. The ball had become deeply lodged in his chest, and to any offers of surgery he replied that he was tired of life and that he did not want any attention.

By the last week of November, William Herbert was fit enough to stand trial in the Central Criminal Court before Mr. Justice Hawkins. The Defence Counsel attempted to prove that the prisoner was insane. They claimed that the intense disappointment of not receiving the enormous fortune had completely upset the prisoner. They also reminded the court that the evidence had shown that no impropriety had taken place between the prisoner and the deceased woman and therefore no motive could be attributed on those grounds. The discovery of laudanum in his pocket was claimed by the Defence Counsel to be proof of his suffering from suicidal mania.

Mr. Justice Hawkins in his summing up reminded the jury that every person was supposed to be of sound mind until the contrary was proved, and the onus of proof of insanity was cast upon the person accused.

At the conclusion of the trial the jury had a short deliberation without leaving the box and delivered a verdict of Guilty of Wilful Murder. Mr. Justice Hawkins told Herbert that he had committed a crime, as far as he could see without a single extenuating circumstance. He then proceeded to pass the sentence of death.

The prisoner was unmoved during the sentencing and he left the dock without displaying any emotion. In the days leading up to his execution he declined any visitors, spending his time in religious devotions. Towards the end he acknowledged the justice of his sentence, and on a Monday morning in December, 1880, he was despatched into eternity by executioner William Marwood. Later that day his remains were buried within the precincts of Newgate gaol.

# Cruel Killing of Constable Cole

On the first day of December, 1882, shortly after nine o'clock in the evening, George Cole, a constable in the Metropolitan Police, left home and went on duty. That night the young married officer was assigned to duty in the Ashwin Street area of Dalston and, wearing his great coat, helmet, belt and truncheon, he conscientiously patrolled the streets.

P.C. Cole had been on duty barely an hour on that foggy evening, when he spotted the figure of a man crouched behind a low wall that fronted the Baptist Chapel at the corner of Ashwin Street and Beech Street. Suspecting that the man had been attempting to effect an entry to the chapel, the constable immediately closed with him. At once the man reacted by producing a pistol and began to fire at the policeman. Two bullets flew past the officer and into the brickwork of neighbouring houses and a third bullet struck P.C. Cole's truncheon. In the next instant the constable slumped to the ground as a fourth bullet penetrated his skull behind the left ear.

A woman named Bucknell, who had seen the constable gunned down, ran from the scene into Dalston Lane from where she fetched two other constables. When they arrived at the spot they saw P.C. Cole lying in the gutter and immediately arranged to have him carried to the nearby German Hospital. Alas, surgical aid was to no avail and the 27-year-old constable was declared to be dead on arrival.

An immediate search was made of the vicinity of the crime from which the culprit had fled. According to witnesses the man was of medium height and had been wearing a black overcoat and light trousers. In his haste to depart he had left behind his soft felt 'wideawake' hat, and over the wall, by the side of a window of the Baptist Chapel, the police discovered a 1¼ inch cold chisel and a cabinet maker's wooden wedge. Examination of the chisel showed that scratched upon it were the letters 'rock' and other scratches which could not be deciphered.

It was concluded that the killer had been disturbed in an attempt to enter the Chapel through a window. When the inquest was held a verdict of 'Wilful Murder' was recorded against some person or persons unknown. Bills were issued offering a reward of £200 and giving a description of the person who had fled the scene on that foggy night.

Despite the efforts of the police very little information was forthcoming and weeks turned into months without the culprit's detection. At last, early in 1884, the police received information that two men named Evans and Miles, had been in the company of a man called Thomas Henry Orrock on the night of the crime, and that they could implicate him as the guilty party.

When this information came to light, Orrock was, in fact, in prison at Coldbath Fields, having been convicted of burglary for some other unrelated crime. Interviews with Evans and Miles revealed that they had been drinking with Orrock on the night of the murder. They both claimed that he had told them of his intention to break into the Chapel and to steal the sacramental plate. Orrock had been a regular visitor to the Chapel where, in fact, he occupied a seat for which he paid. According to the testimony of the two men, Orrock had been in possession of a revolver and the chisel found at the scene.

Later investigations were to show that the revolver had been purchased in October, 1882 by Orrock from a private house in Vicarage Road, Tottenham, following an advertisement in *Exchange and Mart*. After purchasing the revolver, Orrock had gone to Tottenham Marshes and practised with the gun by firing at a tree. The exact tree was located by the police and a bullet embedded in the trunk was deemed to be similar to the one which struck P.C. Cole the fatal blow. The chisel, it was revealed, had been sent by Orrock to a woman for grinding and while it was in her possession, she had scratched the name Orrock on to it, for identification. The letters 'rock' still being distinct on the tool.

When confronted with the evidence, Orrock, a 21-year-old cabinet maker, denied the crime, but in the middle of September 1884 he stood trial in the Central Criminal Court before Mr. Justice Hawkins.

Amongst those called to give evidence was his sister who stated that at the time of the crime Orrock was living with her and that on the evening in question he had returned home between ten and eleven o'clock. His trousers had been torn at the knee and he had explained to her that he had been fighting. Although much of the evidence came from witnesses of 'dubious character', the testimony against Orrock was overwhelming. To the public view he had been a member of the Chapel and Bible class, worthy of respect, yet he had attended Chapel on the day of the murder with the intention of unlatching a window to facilitate his later entry, and on the day of P.C. Cole's funeral he had joined the many mourners.

Two days of court proceedings ended with the Counsel for the Defence suggesting that perhaps it was Miles or, indeed, Evans who committed the crime, rather than Orrock. His claim was that rather than being in the Railway Tavern drinking, the pair were actively involved in the attempted robbery and that they had only offered evidence against Orrock so as not to implicate themselves.

The jury appeared to need little time to reach a 'Guilty' verdict, returning to the court room twenty minutes after their departure. On hearing the verdict, Orrock replied in a firm voice, "I have no more to say, than that I am not guilty".

Mr. Justice Hawkins then assumed the black cap and informed Thomas Henry Orrock that he was to suffer the sentence of death.

Orrock was not to meet his end alone because also committed for execution at the same court sessions was 48-year-old Thomas Harris, a market gardener. He was found guilty of the murder of his wife at Kilburn – having cut her throat with a razor. Both executions were set for the first Monday in October, 1884, at Newgate gaol. After conviction both men were visited daily by the gaol chaplain. Amongst Orrock's visitors were his wife, whom he had married after the murder, his mother, step-father and the minister from the Baptist Chapel.

As his remaining days passed by Orrock appeared to show more penitence and eventually a confession was forthcoming, it being recorded that he admitted to firing the shot that killed the constable, although his only object had been to try and prevent his arrest. On the Sunday night both condemned men retired to rest at 10 o'clock, and they rose at six o'clock in the morning, for their final hours. The Sheriffs had engaged James Berry from Bradford to carry out the executions and he went to the cells with the execution party to carry out the pinioning process.

As eight o'clock approached, the bells of the neighbouring St. Sepulchre's began to toll and the procession moved to the place of execution in the prison yard. The convict Orrock was first placed upon the drop and after him followed Harris. Both men conducted themselves with calmness and fortitude as they stood with the nooses around their necks. A signal was given as the hour arrived and, touching a lever, the executioner sent the men into eternity.

A drop of 7ft. 5ins. was allowed, and death in both cases appeared to be instantaneous. A large crowd had assembled outside the gaol from where they witnessed the hoisting of the black flag.

# Poisoner Elizabeth's Cry of Innocence

From the age of fourteen, Elizabeth Fenning earned her living as a domestic servant. A keen and willing worker, she eventually secured the position of cook in the employment of Mr. Orlibar Turner in January 1815. By then in her twenty second year, she was responsible for all the meals served in the family home in Chancery Lane, London.

Her new position seemed to suit Eliza and all was well until her mistress, the daughter-in-law of Orlibar Turner, caught her in her room with the apprentice Roger Gadsden. The mistress, Charlotte Turner, had discovered Eliza in a state of undress and concluded that she had been bent on seducing the youth. When her mistress would not listen to any explanation Eliza seemed to develop a silent and sullen manner in the presence of Mrs. Turner.

Nevertheless, Eliza continued to perform her duties and on Tuesday, the 21st of March, when the brewer had delivered some yeast, she asked her mistress if she could make some dumplings. By three o'clock that day Eliza had prepared the meal of beef steak and yeast dumplings and it was served to Orlibar Turner, his son Robert Gregory Turner and his daughter-in-law Charlotte.

As soon as the meal was over, all those who partook of the dumplings began to feel unwell, all feeling an inclination to be sick and a burning sensation across the chest. Surgeon John Marshall was at once sent for and that night he successfully nursed the family members, the apprentice and Eliza who also complained of feeling unwell. He suspected that arsenic was the cause of the sickness.

The apprentice Gadsden had eaten a piece of dumpling after they had been returned from the dining table. Eliza had pointed out to him that the dumplings were cold and heavy and had said to him, "Don't eat that, it will do you no good".

Next morning, when Orlibar Turner felt a little better, he took the surgeon to the kitchen and showed him a dish. The surgeon washed the dish with warm water and when he decanted it collected half a teaspoonful of white powder. Close examination of the powder showed that it was, in fact, arsenic.

In a drawer in the kitchen, wrapped in paper marked 'Arsenic, deadly poison' was a quantity of powder, and the conclusion was drawn that Eliza had put arsenic in the dough for the dumplings. When quizzed about the dumplings Eliza had been quick to blame the milk used to make the sauce. However, it was discovered that two of those taken ill had not partaken of the sauce.

During the second week in April, Elizabeth Fenning stood on trial at the Old Bailey charged with administering arsenic to Orlibar Turner, Robert Gregory Turner and Charlotte Turner with intent to kill. Mrs. Turner told the hearing that no one else could have had an opportunity of meddling with the dough except the accused. When the dumplings had appeared on the table she had observed that they were black and heavy, instead of being white and light.

*Elizabeth Fenning*

Orlibar Turner's wife, Margaret, was amongst the witnesses called. She had been out when the poisoned meal was eaten, but she related her conversation with Eliza on the preceding day, when she had told her, "It must have been the sauce. Gadsden ate a very little bit of dumpling, but licked up three parts of a boat of sauce with a bit of bread".

The conclusion reached was that the arsenic had been in the dumplings, and when the case was summed up the jury were told to consider by what hand the poison was administered. The evidence was mainly circumstantial, but the jury took only a few minutes to draw their conclusion. They returned with a 'Guilty' verdict and sentence of death was pronounced. Eliza had to be carried from the dock screaming.

The day appointed for her execution was the last Wednesday in July, and sharing her ghastly fate were William Oldfield and Abraham Adams, two more convicted felons.

In the case of Fenning, many had taken up an opinion that her guilt was not clearly established and public curiosity was strongly excited. To her parents, who had visited her on the previous afternoon, and to the last moment, she persisted in her innocence.

As she prepared to climb the steps of the scaffold she was accompanied by the prison chaplain who asked her if she had anything to communicate. She paused a moment and then said, "Before the just and Almighty God, and by the faith of the Holy Sacrament I have taken, I am innocent of the offence with which I am charged".

She then mounted the platform and stood, dressed in white with lace boots and cap, before the gazing multitude. A handkerchief was then tied over her eyes and she prayed fervently. Her fellow sufferers then joined her on the platform and Oldfield, in his own desperate hour, addressed a few words of prayer to the unhappy girl.

At half past eight o'clock the signal was given, and in a short time the drop fell and three more paid the price of nineteenth century justice. After hanging the usual hour, the bodies were cut down and given over to their friends for interment.

That night a statement relative to Miss Fenning's execution appeared in the newspapers:

"We should deem ourselves wanting in justice, and a due respect for Government, if we did not state that, in consequence of the many applications from the friends of this unhappy young woman who this day suffered the sentence of the law, a meeting took place yesterday at Lord SIDMOUTH's office, (his Lordship is out of town), at which the LORD CHANCELLOR, the RECORDER, and MR. BECKETT were present. As full and minute investigation of the case, we understand, took place, and of all that had been urged in her favour by private individuals; but the result was a decided conviction that nothing had occurred which could justify an interruption of the due course of justice. So anxious was the LORD CHANCELLOR in particular to satisfy his own mind, and put a stop to all doubts on the part of the people at large, that another meeting was held by the same parties last night, when they came to the same determination and in consequence the unfortunate culprit suffered the penalty of the law".

On the last day of July, 1815 Elizabeth Fenning's funeral took place. It began to move from her father's house in Eagle Street, Red Lion Square at half past three in the afternoon. Leading the way were a dozen police officers, next came the undertaker immediately followed by the body of the deceased. The pall bearers were six young ladies robed in white and they were followed by the chief mourners, led by the parents. Several hundred people then followed behind, two abreast, and at the rear were another thirty officers of the law.

All the streets were crowded, and windows and roof tops were occupied by those eager to catch a glimpse of the mournful procession as it made its way to the burial ground of St. George the Martyr.

### Postscript
Many doubts existed over Elizabeth Fenning's guilt and, some years later, when a nephew of Orlibar Turner was on his death bed, he was rumoured to have confessed to Eliza's crime. The man in question was said to have been at loggerheads with the Turner family over an allowance due to him. So annoyed had he been that, as the fateful meal was being prepared, he had taken advantage of the servant's absence from the kitchen and, on entering, sprinkled a quantity of powdered arsenic into the mixing bowl.

# Calamity on the
# Hampstead Junction Line

With the coming of the railways, the people of Victorian London were able to travel to the country or the seaside to indulge themselves in life's pleasures. Besides the regular trains, which worked to strict timetables, carrying goods and passengers, the numerous railway companies introduced the excursion train to transport the day trippers. Each year the special trains, increased in popularity and, packed full of passengers, they often operated at short notice.

One line that emerged, to the delight of the city dwellers, was the Hampstead Junction line, which transported thousands of people to Kew, Richmond and Twickenham. The line, which joined the North London line at Camden Road Station, passed through Camden Town and Kentish Town, by Hampstead. It then went on to Kew where it ran close to the South Western line, over which passengers wishing to travel to Richmond were conveyed without the need to change trains.

During the summer of 1861, not only did the ordinary trains fill well but, on the Sundays and Mondays, excursion trains were constantly required. One particularly busy weekend was the first one in September during which a number of special trains were provided to meet the demand.

One of the trains on the Monday was organised by the friends and relatives of the railway officials of the North London Company, who had formed a Society to support the victims of the all too common accidents on the railways. Ironically, that train, packed with people only too aware of the perils of train travel, was to end the day at the centre of a calamity.

The train left Bow at nine o'clock in the morning and picked up excursionists at every station en route to Kew. On arriving at their destination, the passengers had entered into all the enjoyments of rural revelling. The zest of their pleasures being heightened by the brilliance of the day, away from the dense metropolis.

After several hours spent in this joyous and innocent mode of recreation, the hour approached for their return to the city. Every carriage was crowded and the train sped along at over 50 miles per hour.

Whilst they had been enjoying their outing, work had been in progress on the erection of an extensive coal depot adjoining the Kentish Town Station. Throughout the day a train of trucks had been busily engaged in bringing up ballast from Bushey. On this particular Monday the ballast train was worked into the early evening and, after delivering its final load, it was in the process of being slowly shunted off the down line, when the passenger train from Kew was seen approaching at a rapid pace.

The driver of the ballast train had lighted his lamps, and when he saw the other train approaching, he waved a red light and shouted a warning. The driver of the excursion, chartered by the North London Company, blew his whistle in response, but he could do nothing to bring his engine to a halt before a collision took place. It was not yet dark and many people, walking in the fields or looking from the windows of the houses in the Carlton Road, realised at once the tragedy about to unfold, and let out shrieks of terror.

Within seconds the ballast train had been struck midway along its twenty trucks by the engine of the passenger train. On impact the engine leapt from the rails with a half puff, half bellow and went hurtling down the embankment. It dragged after it the three long saloon carriages and an ordinary second class carriage; the other ten carriages remained on the line and shuddered to a halt with the passengers shocked and shaken. The first two carriages jumped clean into the fields where they lay on their sides, one over the other. The next carriage landed with its end upon the second carriage, its coupling irons had not broken and it was secured to the fourth carriage which, half suspended, had its hind wheels stuck in the embankment.

The scene that ensued was heartrending to the extreme, and the groans and shrieks of the wounded and the dying filled the evening air. The inhabitants of the neighbourhood instantly ran to the scene of the carnage and not a moment was lost in rendering assistance to the suffering.

The ends of the first two carriages had been broken by the fall and several of the passengers were at once pulled clear of the wreckage. Many had been lacerated and were bleeding to a frightful extent. A body of policemen arrived in haste, and with the willing volunteers they freed many a man, woman and child from the crumpled carriages. First aid was administered on the spot, and for the many that needed greater medical attention, a fleet of cabs and wagons were provided to hurry them to the nearest hospitals.

By eight o'clock, some thirty minutes after the collision, darkness was beginning to fall and the remains of the brake van, which lay smashed into a thousand fragments, was set alight. The glare it gave lit a desperate scene as many men were engaged in dragging corpses from under the wheels and axles of carriages that had been crushed to splinters. Ladies were hurrying about with linen for doctors to bandage the wounded, and policemen with lanterns kept a path for those carrying the injured to the waiting transport, which formed a line to the by-road leading to Kentish Town.

The dead and the dying were conveyed to the various hospitals. Six victims, including a ten year old girl, were taken to the London University Hospital; three youths were dead on arrival at the Middlesex Hospital, including two brothers whose father was an official of the North London Railway Company; at the Royal Free Hospital a woman in her early forties died from a fractured spine and at St. Pancras Workhouse an elderly woman passed away from her injuries.

Long after midnight, thousands of people were still at the scene of the wreckage, and the various hospitals and the stations on the line were surrounded by anxious crowds waiting for news of relatives and friends. That night was a tense and long one for all concerned as the medical men attempted to make the injured comfortable and the nurses attended to their needs. The number of injured ran into the hundreds and hospital beds were at a premium.

Early the next morning workmen were engaged in removing the wreckage from the fields and the remnants of the ballast trucks from the embankment. The engine itself lay buried deep at the foot of the embankment and a tramway was to be constructed to pull it back upon the line.

The hospitals were set to be busy for some time, taking care of the injured, many of whom would be maimed for life. As the days passed, the final death toll was to reach sixteen, leaving many families in mourning. By bitter irony, this latest calamity had fallen upon the families and friends of the railway officials and once more called into question the management of the railways.

A ballast train and an excursion train, neither of which had been in the railway time table, had collided close to a station and highlighted the public concern over safety on the railways.

# Shocking Shooting of Isaac Blight

At the beginning of the nineteenth century, there lived in the neighbourhood of Greenland Dock a man called Isaac Blight. To earn his living, he carried on the business of ship-breaker, and occupied a fashionable house with a garden that fronted on to the River Thames.

The family of Isaac Blight consisted of himself, his wife, Sarah, and two children. Over the years a number of domestic servants were employed to maintain the household. In the year 1803, a servant girl was taken into the employ of the Blight household and before she had worked there long, she was visited by her brother, Richard Patch. The girl entreated that he might be permitted to remain a few days in the house, and her wish was granted.

Whilst there, Patch took the opportunity of representing himself to Mr. Blight as a distressed man, telling his sister's master that he had been forced to flee the west of England on account of some pressing demands for tithes. He then begged Mr. Blight to employ him, even in the lowest situation so that he may obtain a livelihood.

In consequence of his petition, he was taken on without salary, but with food and lodgings in return for his industry. He continued under this arrangement for some time until Mr. Blight acknowledged that he was a valuable servant and decided to pay him £30 a year in addition to his board. The new arrangement

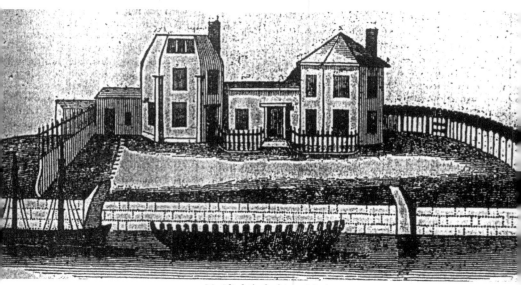

*Mr Blight's fashionable house*

continued for a few months, after which Patch decided it would be more convenient if he lodged elsewhere and Mr. Blight, agreeing to his wishes, advanced his remuneration to £100 a year.

For master and servant all was fine until 1805 when the affairs of Mr. Blight became embarrassed and he was forced to call his creditors together. The outcome being that a Deed of Composition was prepared by which his property was to be made over to the claimants and he was to be exonerated from their demands.

Patch, who was by this time a trusted servant of Mr. Blight, was very active in the drawing up of the arrangements and he and his employer were dealt a blow when one of the creditors did not accede to the conditions and all was thrown into a state of confusion.

Pressed on every side, Mr. Blight resolved to extricate himself in a devious and unlawful manner. In desperation he drew up a document by which he would transfer all his property to Richard Patch. The sum involved was over £2,000 and an understanding was also reached over the lease of the desirable town house. The object was to defraud the creditors and a separate agreement was drawn up between the pair stating that once the creditors had withdrawn, Mr. Blight would return and claim two-thirds of the business, Patch being entitled to the other third share on payment of a sum of £1,250.

The raising of the money proved difficult for Patch who had nothing but his £100 a year income from his service to Mr. Blight. He was determined, nonetheless, to obtain his share of the business and by the due date in September, 1805, he had raised £250 in cash and obtained a bill drawn up for the remaining £1,000. The bill had been supplied by Mr. Goom, a glue maker, but all was not above board and although presented to the bankers, it was destined not to be honoured.

Patch knew of the problem and when Mr. Blight departed for Margate on Thursday the 19th September to visit his family, the servant embarked on a desperate course of action.

That night Patch and a female servant, Esther Kitchener, were alone in the house by the River Thames. During the evening, at the request of Patch, the servant girl was asked to fetch six-penny worth of oysters for supper. Whilst she was away on her short errand a musket was fired, the ball of which entered the window of the front parlour where the Blight family usually spent their evenings.

The explosion occasioned an alarm in the neighbourhood, with Patch dashing to the garden gate in apparent confusion. It was attributed to a malicious intention by some persons unknown. No one was observed in the vicinity of the house despite the quick arrival of onlookers. The next day Patch wrote a letter to Mr. Blight informing him of the discharge of the gun, and suggesting that it had not been an accidental incident but that perhaps one of them had been the object of someone's malignity.

On receiving the communication, Mr. Blight set out from Margate and arrived home early on the following Monday morning. The two men firstly discussed the shooting incident, and then Mr. Blight raised the question of the outstanding money. In consequence, Patch left the house with an absolute prohibition on his return unless he had obtained the cash.

He did not succeed in his endeavours, but he, nonetheless, did return to the house of Mr. Blight and, as the eventful day passed on, master and servant drank tea together and afterwards took their grog.

Whilst the two men were engaged in the back parlour, the servant, Esther Kitchener, busied herself in the kitchen. After about half an hour, Patch entered the kitchen complaining of violent pains in his bowels and asking the servant for a candle and the key to the counting house, which he took off the dresser. The counting house led to the privy and after Patch had left the kitchen, she heard the doors slam behind him as he made his way hurriedly through the house.

Within a few moments the servant was horrified when Mr. Blight staggered into the kitchen having been shot by a pistol in the right hand side of his body. Supporting himself upon the dresser and placing his hand upon the wound, he exclaimed, "Esther, I am a dead man". To which the servant replied, "Lord have mercy, I hope not, sir".

In the next instant Patch was heard knocking violently, demanding admission, and when the servant girl admitted him he assisted his master back into the parlour. Esther Kitchener was distraught and fled the house in order to obtain assistance.

Before too long a couple of neighbours and a surgeon were on hand. The wound was a couple of inches below Mr. Blight's navel and it was apparent to the medical man that the wound was mortal. In consequence he ordered a light dressing to be applied and Mr. Blight to be made comfortable.

Mr. Blight lingered in semi-consciousness throughout the night and before the surgeon departed the next morning, he asked Blight if he had any idea who could have shot him. The victim replying, "No, God knows, I never did any man an injury which could lead him to take my life," and he then added, "Patch has mentioned to me a man of the name of Webster".

The surgeon immediately quizzed Patch in respect of the man Webster and Patch informed him that he was a person suspected of robbing the premises on a previous occasion. However, when the surgeon suggested enquiring as to Webster's movements, Patch responded by saying, "No, for if nothing should be discovered, he would certainly shoot me".

Understanding that Mr. Blight's affairs were not settled, the surgeon then went to his bedside and representing to him his danger, requested him to calm his mind and dispose of his property.

In consequence, the dying man desired that his Will might be brought and, after making some alterations, and making Patch an executor, he signed the document. Subsequently, the surgeon went away, promising to return in the afternoon. He returned at around four o'clock, only to be informed that Mr. Blight had passed away three quarters of an hour earlier.

The investigation in to the shooting of Mr. Blight at once became a murder enquiry, and the suspect, William Webster, was soon eliminated from the enquiries, having been at work, in the presence of others, when the incident took place. Suspicion then began to fall on to Richard Patch and it increased when a law officer examined the privy at Mr. Blight's house and found by the side of the sewer pipe, the ramrod of a pistol. The feeling was that having gone out to the privy, Richard Patch had returned in his stocking feet to fire the pistol at Mr. Blight from the shelter of the partially open door in to the back parlour. The finding of a pair of white, ribbed stockings owned by Patch and which had muddy soles, as if the wearer had walked without shoes, gave further suspicion.

It seemed that Patch had the motive and the opportunity, and that he had planned the killing for some days, having performed the shooting incident on the previous Thursday.

Eventually, the authorities were convinced that Richard Patch was the culprit and during the first week of April, 1806, he stood trial at the Surrey Assizes in Horsemonger Lane. The prosecution case was one of only circumstantial evidence, but this was connected to a series of well ascertained facts.

In his defence the accused had prepared a long statement and this was read out to the crowded court. He claimed that it was impossible for him to have carried out the killing without alerting Esther Kitchener. He concluded with the following words:

"Gentlemen, my fate is in your hands; by your decision I am to live or die. Unhappily, I am not permitted to think of myself only; I have four children, who will be thrown on an uncharitable world in a condition of absolute beggary.

I declare most solemnly, my perfect innocence of the crime and I commit my fate into your hands".

After the Chief Baron had proceeded to sum up the evidence, the jury retired and after only twenty minutes they returned with a 'Guilty' verdict.

Patch was told by the learned Judge that he was found guilty of a crime that had commenced in ingratitude, proceeded in fraud, and terminated in the foul assassination of his friend and benefactor. He then pronounced the sentence of death and stated that after the hanging his body would be delivered to the surgeons to be dissected.

Executioner Jack Ketch was at once engaged to carry out the sentence on the following Tuesday morning. During Monday night the condemned man sat up and prayed fervently in the presence of three Dissenting Ministers, continually asserting his innocence of the crime. Towards morning he refreshed himself with two cups of tea, and then laid down and slept for a short period. When he awoke he asked for a little wine and drank about a glass full.

Shortly before six o'clock in the morning, two prison officials entered the cell and again entreated Patch to make a confession. He, however, contented himself by saying, "I am indeed a heavy sinner; but having confessed my transgressions to God, who alone can forgive me, it is of no use to reveal myself to man who cannot assist me; as it is, I feel myself happy".

Patch was then taken to the chapel where he was joined by a husband and wife named Herring who also awaited execution. The couple were to be hanged for coining and, like Patch, they applied themselves devoutly to prayer.

At nine o'clock precisely the High Sheriff and his attendants arrived at the chapel door and demanded the unfortunate sufferers. First came Herring and his wife, and next Patch followed by the executioner. When they reached the open yard, Herring and his wife were placed in a sledge, according to the sentence of the law on coiners, and drawn to the entrance of the staircase leading to the place of execution. Patch, as he walked along, continued to exclaim in a low voice, "The Lord have mercy upon me!"

The spectators who had been admitted to the prison were allowed to accompany the sufferers to the scaffold platform. On his arrival there, Patch, who was dressed in a full black suit and had on clean linen, became visibly agitated. His awful situation absorbing all his thoughts.

Herring, aged about fifty, and his wife, some ten years younger, were first to be led on to the scaffold, and as they were being tied up the husband seemed more at ease than his wife. Before the cap was placed over his eyes, he called down a blessing on his wife and he kissed her twice.

After another attempt had been made to get a confession from Patch, he was also tied up and the cap drawn over his face. Patch was annoyed at being pressed once again to state his guilt and he showed his dissent with violent motion of his body.

The offenders then stood in the following order – first Patch, then the woman and next to her, her husband. At five minutes past the hour the sentence of the law was carried out by the falling of the drop. Patch's body was convulsed from head to foot, but not violently, and he appeared quite dead inside four minutes. Herring suffered great agony and the executioner deemed it necessary to pull on his legs to terminate his misery. His wife appeared to die instantly.

After the bodies had hung an hour, they were taken down and the body of Patch was conveyed to St. Thomas's Hospital for dissection. The bodies of the other two sufferers were delivered to their friends.

All the public avenues from the Haymarket at Stones End, Newington Turnpike and the bleaching grounds near the Kent Road had been filled with spectators eager to view the executions. Due to the great pressure of people several females had fainted and two men had been trampled in the crush, one being so much bruised that his life was despaired of.

The murder of the ship-breaker had aroused much public interest and word soon spread that the authorities had failed in their attempt to obtain a confession of guilt from Richard Patch.

# Drury Lane Theatre's Real Life Drama

London's famous theatre in Drury Lane has, down the centuries, been the scene of many a gripping drama, with actors and actresses of the highest quality entertaining the theatre-goers of the metropolis. Yet, despite all the theatrical brilliance, the nineteenth century residents of the city would often bring two real life dramas to mind when the theatre was mentioned.

The first incident took place in the month of May, in the year 1800, and the central figure in the drama was no less than His Majesty King George III. On this particular day, the 15th of the month, word spread that the King was to attend a play at the theatre that evening. More than an hour before the start the pit was packed, with late comers crowding in at the rear. The packed auditorium was testimony to the popularity of a monarch who had spent forty eventful years ruling the country.

*The Drury Lane Theatre (19th century print)*

Shortly before the entertainment was to begin, the audience rose to their feet as the King appeared in the Royal Box along with the princesses and the Queen. The Royal Family were greeted by the clapping of hands and the King acknowledged by bowing to his subjects.

Suddenly, a man who stood in the middle of the second row of the pit raised an arm and fired a pistol in the direction of His Majesty. The flash and report caused an instant alarm throughout the theatre. After the awful suspense of a few moments, the audience perceived that the King was unhurt and a cry of "Seize the villain!" echoed through the building. A man who stood alongside the would be assassin immediately collared him and, after a struggle, the pistol was wrenched from his grasp and delivered to one of the performers. The man was then ushered into the music room and into the custody of a couple of Bow Street officers.

*King George III*

To calm the audience, the theatre manager appeared on the stage and told them that the man was safely in custody. The performer who had possession of the pistol held it up to show it to the gathering. The band then struck up "God Save the King" in which they were joined in full chorus by every person in the theatre. The King, who had shown great calmness during the ordeal, was much affected by the loyalty displayed by the audience, and he appeared a little overcome as his family surrounded him.

The man taken captive was James Hadfield, a discharged soldier who had been an orderly to the Duke of York. Six years earlier he had been in battle action for his country and been left for dead after being struck several times on the head with a sabre. His experience had left him scarred, and damage to his brain had left him suffering from strange delusions.

When Hadfield's trial took place he was accused of High Treason. One of the witnesses called was the Duke of York and when the prisoner saw him, he rose from his seat and cried out, "Ah! God bless His Highness, he is a good soul". The Duke recounted Hadfield's military record and related that on interrogation the prisoner had indicated to him that he knew his life was forfeit and that he was tired of living.

Two witnesses told of the purchase of the pistol by the prisoner, and another testified to selling him an ounce of superfine gunpowder on the morning of the crime. A couple of Hadfield's friends stated that on the afternoon of the fifteenth they had partaken of a glass of brandy with him before he had left them to go upon what he described as "some particular business".

The evidence seemed to suggest that Hadfield, fed up of his existence and unwilling to commit suicide, had reasoned that by attempting to assassinate the King, he would, by virtue of the crime, have his life lawfully taken from him.

Many friends and relations were called and their evidence seemed to suggest a man with an unhinged mind. In his world of delusion he had, at times, claimed to be a prince, a king and even the blessed Saviour. On the afternoon of the shooting he had told his wife he was going to a meeting of the Oddfellows and she had encouraged him, believing that such companionship would be good for him.

It was finally concluded that the twenty-nine years old Hadfield was undoubtedly insane and that he could not be found guilty. He was regarded as a danger to society and, as such, could not remain at liberty. When the trial ended he was returned to Newgate gaol and from there he was moved to Bedlam, where he remained.

\* \* \* \* \* \*

The Drury Lane Theatre was forever in the news, as in 1809 when it was destroyed by fire. Londoners felt that they could not continue without the Drury Lane attraction, and by October 1812 a new theatre was ready to be opened.

This latest building was to be the scene of a second headline making incident in February, 1816. Once again a packed audience was in attendance. On this occasion they had gathered to view a farce called *The Merry Mourners* in which Francis Maria Kelly, a young actress, appeared in the character of Nan a country girl, and a Mr. Knight played the part of Joey, a country lad.

While the two performers were embracing, according to their parts, a pistol was discharged from the centre of the pit. Great consternation was excited on the stage and amongst the audience, but the constables of the theatre were quickly alerted and a man apprehended from amongst the crowd. Despite denying that he had fired the discarded pistol, a case of gunpowder was found upon him and the constables secured him with handcuffs.

Several shots had perforated the scenery and it was established that the object of his act had been to shoot Miss Kelly. Fortunately, the woman had been unscathed and, in true theatrical tradition, she continued with her performance to the delight of the audience.

At the conclusion of the farce the theatre manager addressed the gathering in the following manner -

"Ladies and Gentlemen, the young man who fired the pistol has been taken into custody and examined by the Magistrates. From the wild and incoherent manner in which he conducted himself, there is little doubt of his insanity".

On her being informed that her would-be assassin was a George Barnett of Princess Street, the actress recollected that she had received several love letters, some of which contained threats, from a person who had signed them with that name. She, not knowing the person, had treated the whole with indifference, although she had mentioned the letters to the theatre management.

On the second Monday in April, 1816 George Barnett, described as a 21 years old law stationer, appeared at the Old Bailey charged with intent to kill Miss Kelly on the 17th of February.

Miss Kelly was amongst those called to give evidence and appeared much affected and greatly embarrassed by the proceedings. She stated that on the night in question she was performing on the stage. She saw a light, and at the same moment heard what she supposed was a detonating ball, she had not the least acquaintance with the prisoner; had never seen him before that period, nor till this day. At the close of the evidence two letters were produced and read to the court:

### First Letter – "Miss Kelly, Drury-Lane Theatre. Feb. 12th, 1816

Did love ever prompt you to rehearse
The part of honour, unessayed in verse?
Or passion strive to guard it from decay,
Applause to gain, or self-applause to pay?
The works of genius would its charms resign,
And your honour's praise echo every line.
Mistaken girl! ambition would you sway.
To assume a part in each concerted play!
Your Sex's softness endeavour to abuse,
And for defence, not one poor excuse.

I have here, Madam, defined your character and disposition in a few words; and shall go so far as to say, you are not a stranger to my name.

Years ago I was your admirer, but always met with disappointment – coquetry indulged you, though often obtained at the expense of others.

Without vanity to myself, I think my good intentions towards you have been more trifled with than any of my contemporaries; my claim to your person is, therefore, greater, which determines me to demand your hand – or, in other words, to make you my wife.

You will either consent to this, or accept my challenge – I will attend you any hour you please, on Wednesday, or before.

I have witnessed your dexterity in firing a gun, but suppose a pistol will better suit you, as being much lighter.

Had you not infringed the right of your sex, I should not have thus addressed you; but as it is, no other person can better answer this letter than yourself. It shall not brook contempt, or trifling excuses.

GEORGE BARNETT
To Miss Kelly, 22 Princes Street, Drury Lane".

### Second Letter – "Miss Kelly, Performer, Drury-Lane Theatre. Feb. 14th, 1816

Madam, – I received a letter yesterday evening, which, from its apparent rusticity, I believe is your's. You would act wiser if you was to add your name, as I am not sufficiently acquainted with your hand-writing; and, as I hinted in my last letter, not to subject others to be answerable for your forwardness. If the terms specified in my letter were not to your satisfaction, why not express yourself as one becoming your profession? why suffer your temper to overrule your reason?

I love the sex, and once esteemed you as an ornament to it, till you roused my indignation by your impertinence and scandalous abuses.

You are very partial to a disguised male dress; but let me not experience any more of your folly, for if you do, I'll secure you as an impostor, and punish you for your temerity.

I am, madam, your well-wisher,
GEORGE BARNETT"

When asked if he had anything to say in his defence, the prisoner said he had nothing to say. His representatives then announced their intention to call evidence to prove the insanity of the accused.

His mother was called and she stated that her son was the illegitimate child of a waiter at the Piazza coffee house. He had recently seemed very melancholy and low spirited, and on the day of the incident he had appeared very uneasy. She remembered him firing a pistol in the yard on the morning of the shooting.

Many acquaintances recalled his strange manner and behaviour – one spoke of his dancing all night in his room, another of his mocking laughter after the death of a child, another of his habit of sitting in church with his hat on and others of the insane way he spoke of theatricals. A surgeon was also quizzed and he offered the opinion that the prisoner was definitely insane.

When Baron Wood summed up the evidence, he stated that letters bore evident symptoms of insanity and under his direction, the jury declared the prisoner was 'Not Guilty' on the grounds of insanity. He then informed George Barnett that he was a menace to society and told him he would be confined by order of the Crown.

For the second time in sixteen years an outrage at the Drury Lane Theatre had led to an insane man being locked away to protect society.

# A Poisoner Preys on Lambeth's Prostitutes

Nineteenth century folk had a special hatred for a poisoner, regarding him as more sinister than other killers. Known as the coward's weapon, poison has, down the centuries, been used by a number of infamous medical men who administered it with little thought for the lives they had been trained to protect.

Such a man was Doctor Thomas Neill Cream whose activity in the later years of the nineteenth century earned him the title the 'Lambeth Poisoner'. He was born in Glasgow in 1850 and when only two years old was taken by his parents to live in Canada. His father became manager to Messrs. Gilmour and Company, a lumber and shipbuilding firm in Quebec, and young Thomas attended a school provided by the works.

As time went by he was apprenticed to another firm in the district and his father, wishing to see him make his way in the world, entered him in the medical department of McGill College, Montreal. There he matriculated, took his degree and gained some distinction by working on an essay on chloroform.

He had, at that time, been in the habit of going to a place called Waterloo, some 70 miles from Montreal, where he formed the acquaintance of the daughter of a hotel keeper. After one of his visits the young lady was taken ill and her groans disturbed the household so much that the family doctor was summoned. His examination revealed that Neill had, in fact, attempted to procure an abortion. The irate father of the girl immediately proceeded to Montreal and traced Neill to the Ottawa Hotel where, revolver in hand, he threatened to shoot him unless he atoned for his wrong by marrying the daughter.

This Neill readily consented to do, and Rural Dean Lindsey, Vicar of St. Luke's Church, Waterloo, attended and performed the marriage ceremony. The union was not a happy one for the wife was deserted the very next day, with Neill going to Quebec.

In the year 1876, Neill made his first appearance in London and took up residence there with a view to studying at St. Thomas's Hospital. In August of the following year he entered for the examination of the Royal College of Surgeons, but failed to pass. Shortly afterwards he learnt of the death of his wife and in April, 1878, he was successful in gaining a couple of medical qualifications and he returned to Canada.

Taking up a practice in Ontario, he was soon to become involved in a suspicious death. At that place he was often visited by a young woman who was, one morning, found dead in the water closet at the rear of the house with a bottle that had contained chloroform by her side. At the inquest, evidence was given showing that the woman had been seen near the house, but no one had seen her actually enter. Neill, who was not arrested, was called as a witness, and the circumstances were regarded as so suspicious that he was told to leave his practice.

Neill then migrated to Chicago and started a surgery in West Madison Street, where he soon earned an unenviable reputation. An illegal operation on a girl named Julia Faulkner resulted in his arrest on a charge of murder, but he was acquitted.

In the following year, 1881, Neill was advertising a specific cure for epileptic fits and a railway official, Daniel Stott, sent his wife, a young lady of prepossessing appearance, to his surgery for the prescription. Neill, who developed an intimate relationship with the woman, used to send her to a drug store in Clarke Street for the medicine, and on one occasion he added something to the mixture. The result being that the husband died twenty minutes after taking the first dose.

*The cross-eyed Dr Thomas Neill Cream: his bizarre behaviour contributed to his arrest*

In the meantime Neill tried to insure the man's life, but failed. A local doctor was called in and as the deceased had been suffering from fits, he was buried in the usual way. Neill, upon hearing this, telegraphed the Coroner and informed him that the chemist who prepared the medicine had put in too much strychnine.

Getting no reply from the Coroner, he wrote to the District Attorney, who decided to take action in the matter. The body was exhumed and it was discovered that the man had died from the effects of an overdose of strychnine.

Both the wife of the deceased and Neill were then arrested, but the widow gave State evidence against Neill. In consequence, Neill was found guilty of murder in the second degree and sentenced to life imprisonment. He remained in prison until the end of July, 1891. His early discharge was believed to have been due to some pressure on the Government, who commuted his sentence to 17 years, and with good conduct he achieved an early release.

After his discharge Neill went to Quebec and after staying for a time with his brother Daniel, his friends sent him to England.

Returning to London, he again let loose his murderous instincts as he heartlessly led a number of girls to agonising deaths. From October, 1891, he was living at the Anderton's Hotel in Fleet Street and, early in that month, he met a young prostitute called Elizabeth Masters and accompanied her to her lodgings in the Hercules Road, on the south side of the Thames.

Neill spent the evening with her, taking her to a Music Hall and, whilst there, the couple met with a working acquaintance of the girl, called Elizabeth May.

Neill made an appointment with Masters to meet her a couple of days later, but on that occasion, although he was seen in the neighbourhood, he did not turn up. His fickle nature had been attracted by a fresh face and an accidental meeting with another street walker called Matilda Clover.

During the next fortnight Neill was regularly seen by May and Masters in the company of his new acquaintance and, on what was to be the last night of her life, Matilda Clover visited the Canterbury Music Hall with the medical man. Later that night Neill was seen returning with her to her lodgings in the Lambeth Road, at which place he remained for over an hour.

After his departure the girl went back into the streets, returning to her lodgings in the early hours of the morning, apparently the worse for drink. She went to bed immediately and within a couple of hours the household was awakened by her screams of agony. The lodging house servant went at once to her assistance. So terrible was the pain that Matilda Clover was suffering, that when discovered she had wedged her head between the bed and the wall. Her

*Deaths by poisoning meant that the police in Lambeth's New Cut were on the look-out for the killer*

shrieks were awful and she was writhing and screaming. Occasionally, when exhausted, she would clutch her two-year-old babe in her arms.

A doctor arrived at seven o'clock in the morning and, after listening to the landlady's story, treated the case as one of excessive drinking. His visit was short and of little help to the unfortunate girl. In fact, within an hour of his departure she had passed away and the doctor readily issued a certificate, stating that death was due primarily to delirium tremors. In a few days the unfortunate Matilda was buried in a pauper's grave, without a friend to shed a tear over her untimely and painful end. Indeed, she was exposed to the stigma of having died a drunkard's death and so the matter ended, but only for a time.

No suspicion had arisen that foul play had taken place, yet, only a few days after the death, Neill asked his landlady's daughter to inquire as to the death of a girl in the Lambeth Road, a girl with a child, whom he suspected had been poisoned. Still later he wrote a letter to an eminent medical man, accusing him of murdering the girl with strychnine, and in his communication he endeavoured to blackmail the man in exchange for his silence.

For some reason the police took no effective action on the letter, which had been submitted to them, and, in January 1892, Neill paid a flying visit to Canada, having previously become engaged to a young lady called Laura Sabbatini.

In April he returned to London, and soon after public feeling was excited by the death from strychnine poisoning of two prostitutes, eighteen year old Emma Shrivell and Alice Marsh, who was three years older. On an evening in April, Neill had enjoyed a bedroom romp with the girls in their Lambeth lodging house. Before leaving, he had offered each of them three pills for their complexion. The two prostitutes accepted the pills, which were laced with strychnine. Before the night was out they were writhing in agony, and by morning death had overcome them.

During the previous October, a 19-year-old prostitute, Ellen Donworth, had died in similar circumstances in her Waterloo Road lodgings. Her visitor had given her a bottle containing white fluid to drink and, after her agonising death a post mortem had revealed strychnine poisoning.

Intense enquiries were underway and the general description of the person sought was that of a middle aged man who was tall in stature, wore a silk hat, sported bushy whiskers, had gold rimmed glasses and was, in fact, cross-eyed.

Inquiries in to these two cases aroused suspicion concerning the death of Matilda Clover. Two of Neill's earlier acquaintances, Elizabeth Masters and Elizabeth May, were able to state that the same man had been in Matilda Clover's company prior to her sudden death. Her body was at once exhumed and it was diagnosed that she also had been a victim of strychnine poison.

The police were on the trail of the Lambeth poisoner and they, in fact, were aided in the search by Neill's bizarre behaviour. Soon after the two girls had been killed, he wrote a letter to a Doctor Harper accusing his son, who was a medical student, of causing the deaths. The letter was intended as a prelude to blackmail, but the recipient ignored the threats and brought the matter to the attention of the police.

Neill was arrested initially on the charge of blackmail, but the investigations of the police led to the preferment of graver accusations. The evidence was soon stacked up against Neill and included open purchase and possession of capsules; constant association with women of the class from whom the victims were selected; letters accusing innocent people of the terrible crimes; excessive knowledge and interest in the fate of the poisoned girls; personal boasting of his association with the unfortunates and the testimony of a more fortunate girl, Louisa Harvey, who had met him the previous October in Soho and spent the night with him at a hotel. He had believed that he had confined her to an early grave by giving her poisoned capsules to clear her acne. The girl, however, had been suspicious of his intentions and had thrown the capsules away.

The trial of Dr. Thomas Neill Cream took place in mid October, 1892, and with such overwhelming evidence against him, the jury took only twelve minutes to find him guilty. Afterwards Mr. Justice Hawkins pronounced sentence of death, describing the condemned man's crimes as "fraught with cold-blooded cruelty and of unparalleled atrocity".

Whilst Neill awaited execution, he was kept under the watch of two warders night and day because there was a belief that with his medical knowledge he may attempt suicide. However, one leading officer who had been engaged in investigating the wretched crimes said, "He is utterly reckless of other people's lives, but he is particularly careful of his own neck. He does not mind how many he kills, but he certainly won't kill himself".

For similar reasons it was thought most unlikely that Neill would confess to his crimes as long as a ray of hope remained that something may occur to grant him respite and cause delay.

One bright, pure figure in the case, that was otherwise wholly loathsome, was the figure of Miss Sabbatini, the girl whose true, enduring affection for the prisoner had so repeatedly been made apparent. A number of their letters to each other were published at the time and in one Neill wrote, "I am glad you are sticking by me, for if you ever left me, I would gladly lose my life". In a will made shortly after their engagement Neill had made Miss Sabbatini his sole heir, but in a will made after his conviction his solicitors were set to benefit substantially as compensation for the expenses incurred in defending him. The London agent of a leading showman in America was also in touch with the solicitors, a cable being received offering £250 for the condemned man's personal effects.

On Tuesday the 14th of November, 1892, Thomas Neill Cream was awakened in his cell at six o'clock, after spending a restless night. He washed himself and waited for his last meal which consisted of tea, bread and butter, and two eggs. The meal was served in the cell, but it was left practically untasted. Just before being pinioned, however, he was supplied at his request, with a little brandy.

His weight was said to be 12stone 4pounds, indicating that he had put on a few pounds since his conviction. In consequence, a drop of five feet was allowed by the hangman, Billington. On his way to the scaffold Neill Cream walked with a firm step. The culprit wore no collar and was without his spectacles.

The executioner acted with great coolness and promptitude and on the bolt being withdrawn, the drop fell, and the doctor disappeared from view of the spectators in the gaol yard. Death was believed to have been instantaneous and a crowd of two thousand waited outside Newgate gaol for the hoisting of the black flag.

After the body had hung for an hour, it was cut down and an inquest was held. The jury viewed the body, which was lying in a deal shell placed across the drop. It was attired in a new suit, consisting of black jacket and vest with dark blue trousers. The only indication that the convict had met a violent end was the mark of the rope on his neck. Formal evidence having been given, the jury returned its customary verdict.

*Hangman James Billington allowed a drop of five feet for the victim*

The diabolical doctor's life ended without any official confession of his crimes, although his braggadocia had left many believing he had taken the lives of numerous unfortunate females. It was said that his conviction had met with universal approval and that no criminal doomed to death had evoked less public sympathy.

# Robbery and Violence on the Aldgate Line

In the month of August, 1880, Clarence Lewis, an employee of Messrs. Barham and Marriage, tea dealers of Aldgate and Kensington, was destined to make the newspaper headlines after a terrifying train journey from Kensington railway station to the firm's Aldgate establishment.

The eighteen-years-old apprentice was sent every Saturday evening to the firm's Kensington branch to collect the day's takings and deliver them to the Aldgate premises. The practice was an established one carried out by the company and was common knowledge amongst the tea dealer's employees and, indeed, former employees. One such former employee was 24-years-old Henry Perry who, landing on hard times, decided on the third Saturday of the month to snatch the takings from the young apprentice. To this end, Henry Perry made his way to Kensington railway station to await the arrival of Clarence Lewis. On this occasion the apprentice tea dealer had been entrusted with a total of £105 made up of cheques and gold, which he had placed in his trouser pocket in a bag.

As Clarence Lewis boarded the train, he was joined in the first class compartment by Henry Parry who introduced himself and had a laugh and a joke with him over some girls in another portion of the train. After they had travelled a short distance, Perry produced a bottle of mineral water and invited Lewis to try it. The liquid had a bitter taste and Lewis almost choked after swallowing a small amount. Perry then produced another bottle and, pouring some of this liquid on to a handkerchief, he requested that Lewis smell it. The apprentice said he would rather not, and he also refused an invitation to partake of some port wine which Perry produced.

Further down the line a lady joined the two young men in their compartment, an act that appeared to cause Perry some annoyance. However, the woman disembarked at the Kings Cross station leaving the pair alone again on their travels. A few minutes later, as the train was about to head into a long tunnel, Lewis stood up to lean out of the window. As he viewed the line ahead, his travelling companion pounced. Lewis received a violent blow on the back of his head and he slumped to the carriage floor. Armed with a stick, Perry was intent on rendering the youth senseless and further stunning blows were delivered. Then, as Lewis cowered helplessly beneath him, Perry delivered a series of kicks to his victim's body.

Despite spirited resistance the youth was eventually forced to hand over the bag of money his assailant desired, after which Perry, showing little regard for his victim, opened the carriage door and attempted to force Lewis out of the moving train on to the line below. The apprentice begged Perry to relent and in response his attacker made Lewis lie under the carriage seat.

When the train slowed down on the approach to Aldgate Street station, Perry jumped out of the carriage and hurried along the platform. The apprentice immediately crawled out from beneath the carriage seat and as he landed on the platform in a battered and bloodied state, he cried out, "Stop thief". His shout was heard by a bricklayer, John Bell, who had been travelling by the same train, and he at once leapt from his carriage and took a hold of Perry.

The commotion alerted the railway officials and as they approached Perry, he dropped the bag containing the money. His hands were smeared with blood and Lewis, who was in a poorly state, charged him with robbery.

A police constable was soon on hand and when Perry was taken to the police station and searched, two bottles were taken from him that contained some fluid. Examination of the contents showed that one contained chloroform and the other port wine mixed with laudanum. The prisoner's shirt and coat were stained with blood. An examination of the railway carriage led to the discovery of the stick used in the beating and it bore traces of hair and blood. The cushions, floor and door of the carriage were also smeared with blood.

*St. Bartholomew's Hospital – to where Clarence Lewis was rushed after his beating*

The beating handed out to Lewis had been a severe one and he was taken quickly to St. Bartholomew's Hospital in a partially insensible state. There were several cuts on the back of his head, and it was almost a fortnight before he was considered well enough to return home.

The trial of Henry Perry took place in the middle of September at the Central Criminal Court before Mr. Justice Stephen. After being charged with intent to murder and with robbery, the accused entered a plea of 'Not Guilty' to both charges. The evidence against Perry was overwhelming and his Counsel were, at the end, left pleading for leniency on the prisoner's behalf. The jury did not find it necessary to retire to consider their verdict and, after a brief consultation, declared that Perry was guilty of robbery with violence.

Mr. Justice Stephens told the prisoner that he had been convicted of one of the worst offences that had ever come to his knowledge. He had, in His Lordship's

*In keeping with tradition, thirty lashes were ordered for Henry Parry*

opinion, resorted to the most brutal of violence in order to obtain possession of the money.

When asked if he wished to speak before sentence was passed Perry stated, "I am guilty to a certain extent, but I did not mean to hurt him". The Judge then told the prisoner that it was his duty to pass a sentence which would give him some idea of what physical suffering was. In conclusion he announced that the sentence was one of thirty lashes from a cat o' nine tails and a period of twenty years in penal servitude.

On hearing the sentence, the prisoner was stunned and he was removed from the dock in an apparently fainting condition.

# Dreadful Dark December Days

The City of London and, indeed, the whole nation was horror stricken by a series of murders that took place in the very heart of the capital towards the end of the year 1811. The drama began close to midnight on the first Saturday in December when Mr. Marr, a respectable draper with a lace and pelisse warehouse at 29 Ratcliff Highway, was shutting up his premises.

The young tradesman, who had been married about eighteen months, decided to treat his family and instructed his female servant to purchase some oysters for their supper. The girl left the shop door ajar, expecting to return in a couple of minutes, but, unfortunately, the nearest oyster seller had disposed of his stock and she was obliged to go farther on her errand.

On her return, some twenty minutes later, she rang the doorbell repeatedly, but received no reply from within. This alarmed her and she communicated her fears to a neighbouring shop owner named Parker. The man at once assisted her by obtaining entrance to the premises by the back way.

The spectacle that greeted Parker when he went inside the warehouse was such that he was petrified with horror. Mr. Marr was found lying near the window, his lifeless body having been battered about the head. His wife, Celia, who it seemed had rushed to his aid from the cellar, was discovered deprived of life and with her head shockingly mangled. The shop boy, James Biggs, to all appearances had made more resistance then the rest, for the counter, which extended the whole length of the warehouse, was found bespattered with his blood and brains from one end to the other. The body of the unfortunate youth lay prostrate upon the floor, weltering in his gore. Nor had the work of the blood-thirsty assassin stopped there. Even a child in the cradle, only four months old, in its infancy and innocence, had been a victim of the barbaric hands. It was discovered with its throat cut from ear to ear as a final example of a cruel killer's work.

With such silence had the murders been committed that not the least noise had been heard by the neighbours. The watchman on the beat had, shortly after twelve o'clock that night, examined Mr. Marr's window shutters and, on finding one unsecured, had called out to the occupants of the shop. He had received an acknowledgement from within of, "We know it". The belief was that the murderer had been the one to reply, after the completion of his work of death.

The ringing of the watchman's bell had supposedly led the perpetrator to flee without taking any property, and, in his haste, he had left behind the instrument of death, an old iron headed mallet such as a carpenter would use.

It remained a matter of conjecture whether the villain or villains rushed in at the door whilst Mr. Marr was shutting up shop, or got in through the rear of the warehouse. The belief was that the first object had been to destroy the whole family, and the feeling was that the servant owed her life to the fact that she had been sent on the errand.

The Magistrates made every effort to find the killer and several persons were taken into custody and examined at the Shadwell Police Office. Nothing of a guilty nature transpired against them and they were quickly discharged. The Government was quick to act, and within hours a notice was posted in the neighbourhood of Ratcliff Highway and other parts of the City.

"Whitehall, Dec. 12th 1811
Whereas it has been humbly represented to his Royal Highness the PRINCE REGENT, that the dwelling-house of Mr. Timothy Marr, No. 29, Ratcliff Highway, in the parish of St. George, Middlesex, man's mercer, was entered on Sunday morning last, between the hours of twelve and two, by some person or persons unknown, and that the said Mr. Marr, Mrs. Celia Marr his wife, Timothy their infant child, in the cradle, and James Biggs, a servant lad, were all of them most inhumanely and barbarously murdered: his Royal Highness, for the better apprehending and bringing to justice the persons concerned in the said atrocious murders, is hereby pleased to offer a Reward of One Hundred Pounds to any one of them (except the person or persons who actually perpetrated the said murders) who shall discover his or their accomplice or accomplices therein, to be paid on the conviction of any one or more of the offenders, by the Right Honourable the Lords Commissioners of his Majesty's Treasury.
R. Ryder"

The Magistrates were busy in their endeavours and the next day a local carpenter and a servant girl were quizzed by them. Both were able to satisfy the authorities of their innocence and had alibis of a secure nature. When the Coroner's jury sat at the inquest in to the deaths, they delivered a verdict of 'Guilty of Wilful Murder against some person or persons unknown'.

The interment of Mr. and Mrs. Marr and their infant son took place on the following Sunday at St. George's Church in the East. An immense crowd attended and the utmost decorum prevailed.

When the mourners left the graveside little could they have imagined that within a few days another family was destined to suffer the same horrid death. Before the horror excited by the mysterious and barbaric killings had subsided, the neighbourhood in which the victims had resided was once again to become a scene of confusion, horror and dismay.

On the following Thursday night, shortly after eleven o'clock, the neighbourhood of New Gravel Lane, Ratcliff Highway, was alarmed by the most dreadful cries of "Murder!". The scene of the commotion was the 'King's Arms' public house which was kept by Mr. Williamson and his wife and where also resided an old woman, who collected pots and waited in the tap rooms; a fourteen- year-old girl their granddaughter; and, a man named John Turner, who was a lodger.

That night, a little before eleven, Turner came home to his lodgings and after wishing his landlord and landlady a goodnight, went upstairs to bed. Mr.

Williamson, at the time, was preparing to close the public house. Turner, almost immediately upon climbing into bed, fell into a sound sleep, in which he continued for about half an hour. His slumbers were halted by a noise below stairs. He listened for a few moments and then heard the servant-maid cry out, "We are all murdered".

Not knowing what was the matter, he stole downstairs in a state of undress and cautiously looked through the tap-room door, which had a glass panel in it. The first thing he saw was a man dressed in a drab, shaggy bearskin coat, stooping over the body of Mrs. Williamson, which was lying by the fireside. He could not see what the man was doing, but he heard the jingling of coins and supposed he was rifling her pockets. His ears were then assailed by the deep sighs of a person in the agonies of death.

Terrified beyond description, he at once ran upstairs to the top of the house with a view of making his escape. In his fright, he could not find the trap door to the roof; he, therefore, returned to his own room, threw up the window and, tying the sheets of his bed together and fastening them to the bedpost, he descended safely to the ground. The night watchman who happened to be passing at that moment received him into his arms.

The neighbourhood was immediately alarmed and several people soon assembled outside the public house. The door was knocked at and when no answer was forthcoming, it was broken open with a crowbar. Upon entering the tap room, the bodies of Mrs. Williamson and the maid, Bridget Harrington, were found besmeared with blood and lying with their heads towards the fireplace. The head of the latter was almost severed from her body and the skull fractured in such a manner that the brains protruded. Mrs. Williamson has also had her throat cut and her head was very much shattered.

Those who entered then went downstairs and, upon entering the cellar, they found the body of Mr. Williamson lying lifeless with a long iron bar beneath him. His throat was dreadfully cut on the right side. The wound appeared to have been made in the front of the neck by some stabbing instrument and afterwards enlarged whilst the instrument remained in the first incision. His hands were dreadfully hacked and cut, one of his thumbs being completely severed from his left hand. His right leg had received a compound fracture, the bones of it being visible through his stocking. From his general appearance it was evident that he had made a vigorous effort to thwart his killer. The iron bar beneath him was stained with blood and it appeared to have been wrenched from a window in the cellar.

The watchman, accompanied by the others, then went upstairs to ascertain whether any other person had fallen victim to the assassin. Fortunately, they found no one except the landlord's granddaughter who had been in a profound sleep all the time that the murders were being committed.

John Turner, the lodger; George Fox, the first to enter the house; the night watchman and the young girl were examined before the Magistrates, but scarcely anything of significance transpired from the interrogation. Turner was, however, able to give a description of the intruder he had seen, stating that he was about six feet in height, stout and well made and that he carried a thick stick with a knob on the end of it, under his left arm.

A man called Stroud told the Magistrates that shortly before eleven o'clock he had called at the public house for a pint of beer and that when he entered he had observed a tall man in a great coat lurking about the door. Whilst buying his beer he had informed Mr. Williamson of the stranger, and he had replied that he had been there for two or three hours.

The house of the Williamson family was not two streets distance from the home of the murdered Marr family, and to the rear of both of the houses was a large piece of waste ground belonging to the London Dock Company. In both instances it was felt that this land had been particularly favourable to the escape of the killer.

Several persons were examined at the Shadwell Police Office and a number of officers were sent out with pistols and cutlasses to scour the vicinity of Shadwell. The patrols continued each night and every suspicious person who could not give a satisfactory account of themselves was remanded for questioning.

During the weekend, a seafaring man named John Williams, underwent a long and rigorous interrogation. The suspicion against him was built on the fact that he had been seen at the 'King's Arms' early on the night of the killings; that he had returned to his lodgings that evening at around midnight; and that prior to the murders he had no money, but when taken into custody he had a great deal of silver.

The fact that he was short in stature and had a lame leg did not deter the Magistrates from their belief in his possible guilt, although they had been given descriptions of a tall figure at the scene of the crime. Williams claimed that he had been to several public houses on the night of the crime, along with a female acquaintance whom he had met after visiting the 'King's Arms'. In their wisdom the Magistrates decided to detain him for further examination.

As a result, on Christmas Eve John Williams was taken to the Cold Bathfields Prison to await committal proceedings. The twenty-seven-year-old suspect was placed in a re-examination cell and an iron was placed on his right leg. He was allowed to wear his own clothes whilst being detained and had a smart appearance, wearing a brown great coat

*John Williams, a sea-faring man, underwent a long interrogation*

lined with silk, a blue waistcoat, striped blue pantaloons, brown worsted stockings and shoes. He often chatted to the turnkeys during the day, and when one of them told him he was in an awkward situation he replied that he was not guilty and that he hoped the saddle would be placed on the right horse.

A couple of mornings after Christmas, when the turnkey went to Williams's cell, he was horror-stricken to find him suspended by the neck from an iron bar which ran across the cell and from which inmates hung their clothes. He was quite cold and lifeless and his coat and shoes had been discarded. The night before, when he had been locked up, he had appeared tolerably cheerful and spoke confidently of being liberated by the Magistrates.

Despite the death of Williams, the authorities still proceeded with the examination of witnesses in an attempt to establish his guilt. A fellow lodger by the name of John Harrison was called and he claimed that Williams had been acting strangely since the murder of the Marr family. The morning after that atrocity he had observed that Williams's stockings had been muddy, and that following the later murders Williams had returned with muddy shoes.

Landlords and landladies from various local taverns were called to testify as to the behaviour and the company that Williams kept. The accounts suggested he was an unwelcome and unsavoury character, but there was little direct evidence to establish his guilt.

Later that day a Coroner's inquest was held at the prison and the surgeon of the gaol testified that Williams had died from strangulation. Turnkeys and fellow prisoners gave their view of the events and then the Coroner, Mr. Unwin, addressed the jury in the following manner:

"The miserable wretch; the object of the present enquiry, was committed here on suspicion of being one of the perpetrators of the late alarming and most inhuman murders and that suspicion is greatly increased by the result which has taken place; for how much augmented is the suspicion of guilt against a man, who to escape justice has recourse to self destruction.

I have applied my attention to the conduct of those entrusted with the custody of the wretched man, as a subject interesting to the public mind, and I leave it with you. I think there is no culpability attaching itself to them.

It only therefore remains that we consign the body of the self murderer to that infamy and disgrace which the law has prescribed; and to leave the punishment of his crimes to him that has said, "vengeance is mine, and I will repay'".

In consequence of the Coroner's words the jury delivered a verdict of *felo de se*. On the last day of the year the body of John Williams was removed from the prison and taken to St. George's Watch House near the London Docks. The Magistrates spoke to government officials in order to obtain permission to publicly exhibit the body of Williams in the neighbourhood of the shocking crimes.

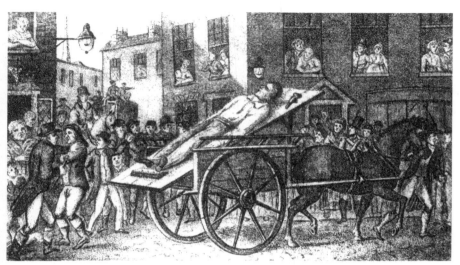

*The body of John Williams was pulled through London's crowded streets*

At ten o'clock the following morning the body was placed on a platform, erected six feet above a very high cart, which was pulled by one horse. The corpse was dressed in a clean white open neck shirt and the hair was neatly combed and the face clean washed. The lower part of the body was covered with a pair of clean blue trousers and brown stockings, without shoes. A mallet, a ripping chisel and a crowbar, all believed to have been used in the commission of the crimes, were placed alongside the body.

The procession, which included over two hundred constables, most with drawn cutlasses, moved through the streets at a slow pace. When they reached the house of the Marr family in Ratcliff Highway, they stopped for quarter of an hour. The procession then went down Old Gravel Lane, along Wapping High Street and continued slowly until the scene of the second atrocity was reached. After another fifteen minute interval, the entourage continued their journey.

Once again the cart and its contents entered the Ratcliff Highway and passed along it until the new cross road in Cannon Street was reached. A large hole had been prepared and, after a pause of ten minutes, the body was thrown into its infamous grave, the interment being witnessed by thousands of spectators and they cheered as the corpse fell. Then in accordance with the law, after the body was consigned to the earth, a wooden stake was driven through it.

The grave was then filled with quick lime and the spectators quietly dispersed. The body of the alleged killer being laid to rest close to the turnpike gate in the Cannon Street Road.

# Also from Sigma Leisure:

## The Charlie Chaplin Walk
*Stephen P Smith*

Explore the London streets of Charlie Chaplin's childhood in a chronological tour that can be taken on foot or from the comfort of an armchair. This book concentrates on the story of Chaplin's formative years and takes a fresh look at the influence they had upon his films. For fans of Chaplin, those interested in film history and anybody with an interest of the social history of London's poor of the late Victorian and early Edwardian era.
*£9.99*

## Crime and Punishment in Derbyshire
## over the centuties
Peter J Naylor

Crime fascinates us all, particularly murders, and the bloodier they are the better they are received. It would appear that the Peak District was a lawless place until more recent times. This book is a thorough mix of most of the types of crimes committed in Derbyshire over the centuries. Each chapter is dedicated to a different type of crime and the punishments handed out. Whilst this book gives much of its space over to murder, other crimes are also included.
*£8.99*

All of our books are all available through booksellers. For a free catalogue, please contact:

**SIGMA LEISURE, STOBART HOUSE, PONTYCLERC, PENYBANC ROAD AMMANFORD, CARMARTHENSHIRE SA18 3HP**
Tel: 01269 593100   Fax: 01269 596116

info@sigmapress.co.uk     www.sigmapress.co.uk